GW00648523

# A Chinaman in my Bath

*By the same author*

BOOKING THE COOKS
Published by Kenneth Mason, 1969

# A Chinaman in my Bath

and other pieces

by

Lord Mancroft

BACHMAN & TURNER

LONDON

First published 1974
by Bachman & Turner
11 Smith Street
Chelsea, London, SW3 4EE

ISBN 0 85974 010 2



Printed by
The Barleyman Press, Bristol
and bound at the Pitman Press, Bath

*Dedication*

Mr. Robert Turner came to my father as his Secretary on the 25th September 1910, when he was 17½ years of age. He has been with us ever since and has typed the whole of this book.

*This* dedication is, accordingly, to *his*.

# Acknowledgment

As was the case with my other book, most of the following pieces have appeared in the pages of *Punch*. I am grateful to the Editor, Mr. William Davis, for his permission to reproduce them.

There are, in addition, four pieces specially written for this book. The remainder appeared in *The Times*, *The Director*, *Metropolis*, and *600 Magazine*, to whose editors I am similarly obliged.

# Contents

# 1

# A Chinaman in my Bath

I'M afraid the business orgy is dying out. Round about 10.30 am on the third Wednesday in every month the tea-lady comes into our boardroom, and puts in front of my colleagues the cup of iron filings boiled in tannic acid which they all seem to like. In front of me, however, she sets a pot of Lapsang Suchong China tea, and this, I fear, my colleagues regard as epicene, if not downright decadent, though they are too polite to say so. And that's about as near to an orgy as we ever get in our corner of E.C.4.

Studying, however, as I do, all these stories in the *News of the World* about sales reps whooping it up in Walthamstow, and the Bacchanalian revels that seem to go on after hours in Throgmorton Street, I'm beginning to wonder whether our board isn't missing something.

We have our usual Christmas party in the office, of course, and very enjoyable it is, too. I notice, however, that some companies are dropping this particular celebration. I suppose they feel that there's a risk of an unreflective little frippet from Accounts saying something to the managing director late in the evening which may unbalance the office for weeks to come.

One of our contractors, for instance, tells me that their office party last Christmas was disturbed by a young lady from the typing pool. She rushed into the general office observing, "I've been seduced." Her friends crowded round to give her comfort. "Who could have done this dastardly thing?" they inquired. "Obviously one of the directors," she replied. "Who else would wear an Old Etonian tie, and make me do all the work?"

Business, of course, has been business down the ages, but somehow I think our forebears managed to mix business and pleasure with greater panache than we do. Take the Romans. Petronius has a nice bit in *The Satyricon* about a dinner party given by a neighbour who wanted to acquire a few acres off him at a knock down price. History doesn't relate how the deal went, but it does record that the host kindly provided a little golden-haired slaveboy through whose curls the guests could run their fingers when they had got a bit greasy from the Umbrian chicken legs and ham bones. Now, that's really obliging. I doubt if you could get that sort of service in the Savoy even if you gave them weeks of notice.

Plautus had sensible views, too. In one of his plays he demonstrates that the best way to crack an egg is to place it between the navels of two young Nubian slavegirls standing face to face, and then instruct them to rotate simultaneously. But suppose you are taking out a couple of tough Dutch shipbuilders to lunch at the Ecu de France, you can't just send down to the Brook Street Bureau and ask if they've got a couple of Nubian egg-crackers on the books. They'd have you round at the Savile Row police station in a trice.

And what about the Rape of the Sabine Women? That sort of behaviour wouldn't go down at an English party even in this Permissive Age. Imagine if you were asked to the Ladies Night at the local Rotary Club, and just as they were tucking into the Bombe Surprise you suddenly scooped up all the wives of the Committee, popped them over the bonnet of the Rover, and away home you went to Potters Bar. Well, I mean, you wouldn't be asked again, would you?

I'm beginning to think that the whole of this Wine, Women

and Song stuff is a bit exaggerated as far as British business is concerned. About American business I'm not so sure. What usually happens in fact is that you are taken out to the Tycoons' Club for luncheon to celebrate the deal. To a background of gin and Musak, you're given far tee many Martoonis. You're then treated to a piece of steak the size of the West Riding of Yorkshire (and about as yielding) which you wash down with scalding hot, white, very sweet coffee, and after you've gone down in an elevator which leaves your stomach up on the top floor, you stagger out into Wall Street and send off a Telex to your chairman saying the deal has been clinched, to which he replies, sourly, "Why only three per cent?"

These are the facts. But in legend, ie, in *Playboy* magazine, things turn out differently. The boys take you out to dine in Greenwich Village, and shortly after the Pot Roast has been done with the Maître D wheels in an enormous cake out of which erupts 38-26-38 of very undressed blonde who raises her glass in a bumper toast to the Discounted Cash Flow. This is an entertainment at which I have never actually assisted.

I must confess that I did once go to a Travel Sales Conference at the Coventry Street Corner House where a lady named Princess Ouida Ouigglebelli (or something like that) had been engaged to take off all her clothes slowly and quietly to music. The guests on either side of me expressed the opinion that she was a nice enough girl, though she was constructed on architectural principles too generous for their taste, and that next year they would prefer Morecambe and Wise. I, too, was beginning to wonder whether business and sex really mix.

My Uncle Percy used to drop dark hints about celebrating a successful coup by taking some charming little Thing out to supper in a private room at Rules, and drinking champagne out of her slipper. Even if he did, I believe the operation must have been a great deal more complicated than it sounds. And knowing my Uncle Percy, I bet he made a right mess of it, too. The nearest I've ever been to it myself was during the war when I went to a Hogmanay Party with the London Scottish, where they were reduced to drinking oatmeal stout out of a NAAFI girl's gumboot. The experiment was not a success.

The Russians, of course, have to be different. In their funny Victorian way they still foster the idea of the tired Western businessman relaxing to the sound of throbbing balalaikas whilst the current Mata Hari adjusts the bugging device behind the armoire.

Some while ago I went to Leningrad with a deputation from the British Tourist Authority. On the first night after our arrival the Russian Travel boys threw a party in our honour. It was a fine party (they wanted a good deal from us) and by midnight we were awash in vodka. Knowing that I had to make a speech next day I slipped away to my room, undressed, and went into the bathroom in search of Alka Seltzer. Slightly to my surprise I found an elderly Chinaman sitting in my bath washing his toes. "Hi," I said loudly (in English, of course). To which he replied, "Hi," equally loudly in Chinese, which, in these circumstances, sounds roughly the same. I put on my dressing-gown, and in some confusion ran out into the corridor, and into the welcome arms of my colleagues Lord Geddes and Sir Charles Forte. They led me back to my room explaining comfortingly that I was not drunk but had merely forgotten that in the Astoria Hotel, Leningrad, each bathroom served two bedrooms, and that unless you also locked the other door from the inside you were bound to find someone like an elderly Chinaman in your bath. Relieved, I retired to bed, and slept the sleep of the just.

But at breakfast time next morning our interpreter, Tanya, bore down upon us with lowering brow. We asked anxiously if ought was amiss. Indeed there was. As a matter of fact there had been a diplomatic détente; a démarche, even. It appeared that the Deputy Chairman of the Soil Erosion Committee of the People's Republic of Outer Mongolia had been insulted in his bath by an Alcoholic Nude.

My friends tutted and clucked, but loyally did not give me away. I'm sorry to say that I sat silent in smug content. There could be few international Travel Conferences, I felt, that had ever been addressed by an Alcoholic Nude, and a member of the House of Lords at that.

# 2

# The Natives are friendly

I COULD never aspire to an office so grand as that of the Deputy Chairman of the Soil Erosion Committee of the People's Republic of Outer Mongolia, about whose ablutions I have just been complaining.

Nevertheless, I took a lively pride in the Presidency of the London Tourist Board, from which I have recently retired after ten years in office. I enjoyed the work, and I shall miss the fun.

For nearly twenty-five years I have been connected with Travel and Tourism. For seven years I was spokesman for the Board of Trade in the House of Lords, and had to answer questions about Travel and Tourism whenever they appeared on the Order Paper. I am glad to say that they appeared frequently, and I acquired a keen taste for the subject. In 1958, as gamekeeper turned poacher, I left the Government to become Chairman of Global Tours, which was part of Sir Isaac Wolfson's Great Universal Stores. Global was a pioneer of package tours and also one of the biggest coach-tour operators in the business. At the height of the season we might have had as many as 250 vehicles trundling along the roads of Europe.

After eight years with Global I went across to the Cunard Line as Deputy Chairman, and stayed there until we were taken over in 1971. During this period I also served a couple of stints on the Board of what is now known as the British Tourist Authority. I crossed the Atlantic forty-seven times, and went round the world thrice. The last time round I was strike-bound for four days in Honolulu at Panam's expense. If you *have* to be bound by a strike, that's the way to suffer.

Tourists as a breed can be a rum lot, and Tourism a fascinating source of controversy, as I am sure my successor at the London Tourist Board has by now discovered.

The new President is none other than the Dean of St. Paul's. I have known Martin Sullivan ever since he came back from New Zealand to take up the appointment of Rector of St. Mary's, Bryanston Square, the parish in which we then lived. He's a fine, extrovert and rumbustious character. Any Dean who can put on in his Cathedral a special service for the cast of the rock musical *Hair* is obviously going to have some pretty positive ideas about Tourism. Indeed, he has already made it clear that his attitude towards tourists is "the more the merrier". Well done, that Dean.

In the past two or three years, however, less welcoming voices have occasionally been raised. People have complained that the number of tourists has been increasing at such a rate that the natives can hardly find room to move. The large number of foreign shoplifters has not passed unnoticed. A newsvendor in Piccadilly displays a notice saying "English spoken here"—and he has a point. We are told that it is nearly as difficult to steal the Crown Jewels as it is to see them. Bold spirits have gone so far as to challenge the whole idea of Tourism being good for the economy.

To help accommodate this influx, a large number of grant-aided hotels have been built, some in the provinces but the majority round about Heathrow. A fair number have also sprung up in South Kensington, where there have been muttered comments about the Costa Cromwell Road. Such, however, is the increase in the rate of building that one or two new hotels have already run into difficulties, particularly in the off-peak seasons.

One of the principal tasks of any tourist board is to try and reconcile a conflict of interests. We in London naturally want to welcome as many tourists as possible, but without upsetting the day-to-day life of the City. This is not an easy reconciliation to make, but it is vital that it should be attempted. One of the chief attractions to London, as many visitors tell us, is the friendliness of the average Londoner; it will be a sad day if the natives ever turn sour, and cease to be friendly. We and all the other tourist boards have tried to deal with this problem by extending the season as far as possible, and by trying to persuade visitors to move out of London and off the beaten track.

We've all heard of the fictional tourist who wants to drive round the island in the morning and take in the traditional London tourist sights—the Tower, the Abbey, and Marks & Spencers—in the afternoon. Well, we've done a lot to change his habits. Stratford, Oxford and Edinburgh will, of course, always attract the multitudes. Try as we may it is not easy to persuade tourists to flock to, say, Manchester—which is where one visitor announced he would like to die since the transition between Manchester and death would be almost unnoticeable. But we do try to let people know about the Border country, and the Northumberland coast, and the other less hackneyed parts of Britain. We beg them to go and see for themselves where Constable found his sweeping skies, Cotman his churches, and John Crome his oak-encircled farms. Such a journey would be well "worth the detour" (Baedeker) even though one East Anglian hotel was recently and rather ominously described in *The New York Times* as having "hot and cold running water, English style". And all this had to be done without upsetting the Welsh, the East Anglians and the Northumbrians.

One new tourist problem with which the Dean will have to cope is the Japanese invasion. It has already reached New York, where Japanese hotels and restaurants are springing up like mushrooms. The language problem and a natural herd instinct makes the Jap an unadventuresome traveller. He likes familiar contacts, so I'm afraid it will take us a long time to lure him away from his compatriots, and turn him into a tourist on his own, and an equally long time to lure him off the beaten track. But he's now coming to Britain, and soon he'll be coming in large numbers. So we must start to learn a little more about him, his likes and dislikes. His, not hers: the Jap seems to regard his wife as a hindermeet rather than a helpmeet, and he prefers to travel in male chauvinist packs.

He is, to start with, by no means as inscrutable as we've been led to believe. In private he's exquisitely polite, but in public he can be very brusque. Tread on his toes in the rush-hour and he'll scrute his head off! In some respects, however, he still preserves the quiet philosophy of the Orient. I was driving once in a taxi with Cunard's representative in Yokohama. The driver short-changed him—a thing I hope would never happen in London. He just looked at the coins in his palm and observed ruefully, "Overflow money go adrift."

The Jap tourist in his turn will want to learn a little about the funny habits of the British. He may have a good deal to learn. A Jap courier, for instance, rang us up recently and asked if St. Paul's was open on a Sunday. With a quiet smile we passed that one on to the Dean.

# 3

# Red Carpets & Hope

IT IS better to travel hopefully, Robert Louis Stevenson assures us, than to arrive. I have never yet discovered what induced him to make this asinine pronouncement, though I realise, of course, that he lived before the age of the Jumbo-jet, the Inter-city express, and the T. & G.W.U.

Hope nowadays tends to languish when Trans-Siberian Air-lines regret to inform transit passengers of a further delay in the departure of their flight No. TSA 007 to Samarkand, and that this is due to operational reasons. (Operational reasons are to an airline what virus infections are to a doctor. You are to understand that neither of them has the faintest idea what has gone wrong.)

I doubt if R.L.S. ever had to sit for an hour outside Didcot station whilst British Rail, reluctant to admit that in the winter our weather tends to be wintry, struggled to unfreeze the points.

No amount of graft or low cunning, no friends in high places, nor the lushest of red carpets will get you out of this sort of mess. There are, in fact, two types of red carpet, the one upon which your ego can pose with pride, and the other which may genuinely speed you on your way. The merits of the two must be separately assessed.

The first type of red carpet was designed to be laid up to the carriage door of some prestigious traveller by coach or rail; but even the best laid carpets can go oft agley. The army manoeuvres which King Edward VII attended in Yorkshire during the summer of 1909 had to be cancelled because of the English summer weather, and the King returned to Harrogate station before the arrival of the Royal Train that was to take him across to Sandringham. In his kindly way he tried to put the Station-master at his ease, whilst that embarrassed official peered anxiously down the line, cursing the engine driver beneath his breath. "Tell me," said the King, "what will happen if, when the train does eventually arrive, the driver fails to pull my carriage up against the red carpet laid out here on the platform?" "Ee," replied the Station-master, tried beyond endurance, "Ee, let boogger try!"

Nowadays, the red carpet is seldom seen at railway stations unless you happen to be the sort of person who normally travels with four corgies.

Privileges to a lesser degree, however, occasionally attend a Minister of the Crown. Once upon a time I was such a person, but it always worried me when, as I often did, I boarded a packed Cardiff train only to find that my secretary and I had been allotted an entire compartment to ourselves in order that we might discuss in secrecy the problems of unemployment amongst the slate-workers of Anglesey. No matter how much our unseated fellow travellers shook their fists, mouthed insults, or scribbled obscenities on the steamy windows, the guard refused to let them into our otherwise empty carriage. Some years later the improper thought crossed my mind that the guard, not sharing my political views, may have felt that all this parade of privilege could influence some votes.

That's one of the troubles about red carpets. The advantages they may bring to the beneficiary often seem to be at some other travellers' expense. "Good evening, Sir," says the air-line P.R.O., smiling a P.R.O. smile, "a pleasant trip, I hope. Here, let me take your passport." Since you travel widely and your passport is consequently big with visas, you must appear glad to be relieved of this heavy burden. You are whipped through Immigration at the speed of light, pushing aside elderly nuns and chronic invalids. You are hustled conspiratorially down long draughty corridors, and you naturally reach the baggage collecting area well ahead of the crowd. But your beautiful raw-hide suitcase takes just as long to come out of the bowels of the airport as does the elderly nuns' shabby grip, and all you'll have gained is a swollen ego at the price of some nasty looks.

It's the same on board a ship. You are nearly at New York's Pier 92. The baggage master, with a knowing glance, tells you that all is under control, and the Purser himself is looking after your papers. A private car has been laid on. Someone from the Consulate will attend. But as the ship is about to dock the familiar cry of "Everybody out" echoes along the quay, and a wildcat strike has you all, Duke and dustman alike, in its thrall. When it comes to carpets, the colour red means less than nothing to the unions.

The red carpet, however, means a lot to the ageing film star who needs the publicity, and to the retiring ambassador who has lived on protocol all his life, and wants to savour it for the last time.

Air and shipping lines have a private code with which they mark their manifests, in the same way that a tramp will mark a door for the benefit of the next tramp to come along. If, say, Lord George-Brown, or Mr. Mick Jagger are travelling with us on Trans-Siberian, it will be known to all concerned how they are regarded by Cunard and BEA. Thus the precise way in which the carpet should be unrolled can be the more readily assessed.

A general assessment is fast becoming more difficult to make not because docks, airports and railway stations are growing more comfortable, or their staffs more efficient, but simply because the sheer bulk of modern travel makes it impossible to try and separate the sheep from the goats. When Euston Station first reopened there were found to be no seats for passengers to sit on. This requirement had not in fact been overlooked. It was simply that the authorities didn't really want people to settle down and make themselves comfortable. They wanted passengers to come and go as quickly as possible, and everyone to be equally uncomfortable.

In spite of this bizarre approach the travel authorities will never really run out of red carpet for the maimed, the sick and the blind, provided, of course, that they are given sufficient warning. What is actually wanted is a little less red carpet and a lot more good communication.

Couldn't T.S.A. have told me why my plane was delayed? I, too, am sorry that I was stupid enough to miss it when our flight was eventually called, but I'm not so observant as all those Pakistanis and au pair girls. The public address system is incomprehensible (even in English) and the closed circuit TV screen is practically invisible. And when I arrived, I know I hadn't warned anybody in advance that I'm badly lamed, but I wasn't lame when I disembarked from the aircraft at the end of a very slippery four-mile corridor.

I think all travellers should be regarded as VIPs, and all should be treated to the red carpet. The motto of the Green Star Line was alleged to have been "Passengers must not," and there are still some carriers who regard the passenger as an infernal nuisance rather than as their source of daily bread.

Ideally, then, all carpet should be equally red, and it may have been the unlikelihood of achieving this Orwellian bliss that was at the back of Robert Louis's mind. If, however, that day ever comes there will still be some people who for one reason or another are desperate to work their way to the head of the queue. For them new carpets must be devised, and old egos revalued. To those in urgent need of such preferential treatment, I commend a simple ploy. This calls only for the use of a small child, and the possession of an indelible red crayon.

Apply the latter to the face of the former in a series of irregular blobs. Then rub a moistened finger lightly over the face, in order to ensure uniformity. Grasp the child by the hand, advance boldly through the crowd, looking neither to left nor right, but pointing anxiously at the child whilst muttering the word *Masern*, or *rougeoles*, or *morbilio* or *sarampion* depending upon whether you are hustling through Germany, France, Italy or Spain. At any harbour, station, or airport where English is understood the word "measles" will suffice, and it will prove an equally effective red carpet.

# 4

# Flies under Starter's Orders

IT WAS a long time since I had last been in the Home Office, and I cast a nostalgic eye around the Secretary of State's vast room. A beaming Reggie Maudling came forward to greet me.

For three years, in the fifties, I had served as Under Secretary of State to Gwilym Lloyd-George. He was a very nice man but a very bad Home Secretary and completely under the thumb of Sir Frank Newsom, our formidable Permanent Head. Nevertheless, I had thoroughly enjoyed the work.

"Have a drink", said Reggie, coming to the point at once. "I've got a job for you. You've left Cunard, haven't you, so I want you to take on the Chairmanship of the Tote. I'm sure you'll enjoy it. You've always been interested in horses, you'll meet some amusing people, and your office has a wonderful view of St. Paul's. Oh, and by the way, I'm told that the Tote is bankrupt. Did you say water, or soda?"

"Reggie," I said, "how can a Tote possibly go bankrupt? You take the money in from the punters; you set a little aside for such essential overheads as the Chairman's salary; you then pay out what's left to the lucky winners. How does bankruptcy come into it?"

"Don't stand there asking tomfool questions," said the Home Secretary, "that's exactly what we want you to find out. Get a move on. This is a real challenge."

I'm always suspicious when anything is described as a "real challenge". Crossing Piccadilly is a challenge, drinking carafe plonk in a strange restaurant is a challenge, even staying married is a challenge. I pondered on all this as I wound my way back through the Home Office catacombs. Obviously, holding such an unusual tiger as this by the tail *was* going to be a challenge.

Of course I soon found out why the Tote was in the red. The British Tote is the only one in the world that has to operate in direct competition with 15,000 licensed betting-shops. Very few countries tolerate bookies at all, let alone allow them to operate betting shops. Some countries, Australia and New Zealand for instance, allow bookmakers on the race-course. It is argued, fairly enough, that bookies shouting the odds on the rails adds to the drama and excitement of racing. Punters like to know what odds the market is offering and they enjoy pitting their wits against the book. And the Tote is always there for the quieter customers. But off-course bookmakers are strictly forbidden—except in Britain.

In Britain, only 5 per cent of the bookie's turnover comes from the race-course. The rest comes from the betting-shop and the telephone. Few of the bigger bookies would bother to appear on the race-course if it weren't for the advertisement they gain. The Tote, however, has to operate at every course.

The betting-shop was legalised by H.M.G. in order to do away with the evil of the street-corner bookie, the factory runner, and the corruptible young policeman. I made speeches on the subject when the Bill was going through Parliament, expressing the view that the cash that ought to be finding its way into prize money and the improvement of racing, would now be deflected into the pockets of the bookies. And, for good measure, I pointed out that the Chief Constables had recently expressed the opinion that the bookmaker was at the back of far too much criminal activity for racing's peace of mind. If I'd realised then the damage that the institution of the betting-shop would also do to the Tote, I would probably have mentioned that, too.

Had I also realised that I'd end up one day as Chairman of the Tote, I would probably have expressed all these views in a slightly lower key.

The fact remains, however, that the British punter clearly wants both systems of gambling—Tote and bookie working side by side. Equally clearly, the Government intends him to have them. Tote and bookie have therefore got to get along together. And, although the betting-shop will probably be nationalised one day, it certainly won't be in my day.

Understandably, my appointment received no more than two cheers from the bookmakers' Lobby. Next to the kiddies' Lobby, and the doggies' Lobby, the bookies' Lobby is the most efficient I have ever encountered in forty years of political life. The way in which the bookies rearranged the Tote Bill of 1972 was a model of what legitimate lobbying should be. So in the end the Bill wasn't quite what the Government had intended, or the Tote required.

Since moving into my Chair with the wonderful view of St. Paul's I have naturally given a good deal more thought to horse-race betting, in particular, and to the activities of the gambling bug in general.

It has always been held that the Chinese are the world's greatest gamblers, but I think we British may be overtaking them. This is difficult to prove, because the statistics of gambling are notoriously perverse. The fiver that you take to the race-course may turn over half-a-dozen times before it finally comes to rest in Honest Abe's satchel—or, better still, the Tote's cash-box. But all the indications are that we are leading the Chinese by a short head.

The French are more intense in their gambling than we are. The air of concentration that hangs over the French pavement café when the weekly tiercé is under discussion is greater even than that of the Bingo Hall in Bournemouth. In addition to Bingo, the bookies and the Tote, we have, of course, the pools, as well as a proliferation of casinos, not all of which are smiled upon by the Gaming Board. There is, in fact, too much competition for a French-type tiercé ever to find favour here.

The Americans are headstrong gamblers, and I have seen bill-folds flashed at Hialeah and Belmont that would make our Betting Levy look like pin-money. As for Mr. Howard Samuel's Tote operation in New York, it turned me green with envy. But, sophisticated though it is, it does not service the punter all that much more quickly and efficiently than our own rather Heath Robinson arrangement here.

The Spaniards are emotional gamblers, and knives are drawn upon less provocation than would be acceptable, say, in the Working Men's Club at Cleckheaton.

The Japs not only ban bookies from their race-courses, but women, too.

The Dutch have never recovered from the teachings of their sixteenth-century countryman Erasmus. In his view, gambling was worse than sodomy, but he never explained quite why.

The Jamaicans are rash gamblers, and will bet upon two flies crawling up the wall. Considering the difficulty of getting one, let alone two flies under starter's orders, this appears very rash indeed.

But the British, in comparison, are now almost compulsive gamblers, and this brings problems in its wake. We spend about two-thousand-millions a year on gambling. This is more than we spend on education—and critics of our current student scene may think that this is as it should be. The Government are in a difficult position. The tax on gambling brings in a tidy sum, but the enormous individual fortunes to be won on the football-pools also bring untidy social problems in their wake. So do "Spot-the-ball" contests, so do the shadier casinos, and so do the profits of some of the bigger bookies.

The Churches take a moderate view. Gambling in excess can be a drug. A whisky-and-soda as a night-cap is all very well, but a bottle a day will kill you. So it is with nicotine, aspirin, and even the seemingly harmless Bingo. A modest flutter on the Derby, say the Churches, is acceptable; but it can very easily become immodest. People are obviously going to gamble, anyhow. The Churches—R.C. and C. of E., at least—accept this, and their proposals are designed to keep gambling within reasonable bounds.

The Tote has its problems, too. The new Law now enables us to operate both as a Tote and as a bookmaker at Starting Price odds. Such an operation will hardly commend itself to the bookies, and the competition will be intense.

"I hope you're not going to flaunt yourself now that you're the Government's Turf Accountant", one of the Bishops said to me after the Tote Bill had become Law. I explained to him that we were still on an economic knife-edge, and that it only required a run of bad weather, or bad fields, or bad luck, to push us back into the red. Our competitors, the regular bookies in their betting-shops, wielded a formidable power and expertise. As for flaunting ourselves, though—well, we could hardly meet Reggie Maudling's challenge by sitting back and hoping that business would drift our way. Confucius he say man waste much time standing with mouth wide open waiting for roast duck to fly in.

The view of St. Paul's is certainly splendid, but there's another challenge Reggie Maudling never mentioned at all. The G.P.O. have got our address wrong in the 'phone book.

# 5

# An egg and a prayer

I SEE that General Ralph Haines, the American Commander-in-Chief, summons his Staff every Friday morning to a 6 a.m. prayer-breakfast.

Greatly though I admire both prayer and breakfast, I am glad that I am not on the General's Staff, however reassuring it may be to learn that he regards himself as being on a special wave-length Up There.

The working breakfast is, of course, a more fashionable institution in America than it is over here. British businessmen visiting the States for the first time should be warned accordingly. I was not so warned, and I found myself at 8 o'clock on a blisteringly hot Texan morning with my mouth full of doughnut, trying to explain to the Social Editress of a Dallas evening paper why Prince Albert was Prince Consort and Prince Philip is not.

How the Americans, who in most respects are quite a civilised people, can indulge in such a barbaric ritual as the working breakfast passes my understanding. Their "Brunch", however, is a different matter, and 11 o'clock on a bright Sunday morning in the Plaza in New York is not a bad time or place for putting the world to rights.

Brunch used also to be a popular meal in Victorian Oxford, but it's seldom heard of there today. When I was up at Christ Church in the thirties there was also a function known as the Riding Breakfast. I had joined the O.T.C. Cavalry Squadron—not because I was of a particular martial disposition, but simply because it was the cheapest way to learn to play polo. We foregathered at 6.30 a.m. on Port Meadow, and I used to ride home to breakfast with my Troop Commander, John Hobson, who later became Attorney-General. John's usual breakfast was Guinness and a pork-chop, and he thought me effete for not following his example. His diet, however, looked like nursery stuff compared with what our forefathers used to put away before a day's hunting. Squire Mytton, for instance, liked half a cold partridge washed down by a bottle of claret, having had a plate of figs as a starter. Colonel Wheeler, of the Royal Horse Artillery, preferred steak-and-kidney pudding for his breakfast (not pie, but pudding, with a little brandy poured into it) and he had his man-of-affairs sit beside him, to go through the rent rolls whilst he ate. But our forefathers were made of tough stuff, and people who could set fire to their night-shirts in order to frighten themselves out of the hiccups were not going to be put off by a mere pork-chop.

Lloyd George was a great man for doing business over breakfast. This is not surprising, and is well in character. Ll.G. could charm a bird off a tree, and then sell the tree back to the bird with a 100 per cent mark-up. So when he found that some soldier or statesman was standing in his way, the Prime Minister would invite his opponent to breakfast—a meal at which the poor dupe was probably never at his best, even had he not been at his desk all night. In next to no time the guest would find himself agreeing to do exactly what Ll.G. wanted, although he had arrived at No. 10 determined to do nothing of the sort.

The Borgias also did business over breakfast, though invitations to such meals were probably received with mixed feelings.

The Cardinal Archbishop of Mantua, for instance, was summoned to Rome by Caesar Borgia in the summer of 1498 to settle a dispute about the payment of some Church tithes. He was given a dish of coneys for breakfast, which I should have thought an unwise meal at the height of a Roman summer, even if you weren't the guest of the Borgias. History doesn't relate how the tithe talks progressed, but it does relate that owing to the extreme heat the Cardinal had to be buried the same day. Not even Ll.G. was ever accused of giving elderly clergymen rabbit for breakfast.

Fashions have probably changed in 10 Downing Street, as elsewhere; and breakfast, whether as a domestic or a business event, is in decline. This was borne upon me when I recently saw a revival of Noel Coward's *Hay Fever*. The third act revolves around a monumental row at the breakfast-table. Guests, family, and a much criticised piece of haddock, are all embroiled, and I fell to wondering when I myself had last sat down with seven other people to breakfast.

I exclude breakfast in the train, which British Rail does well—particularly the kippers. The last time I journeyed to Liverpool, the breakfast-car was full—with some forty men and two women. The women discussed proposals for a new fashion magazine, at the tops of their voices; but the men, as far as I could observe, seemed to keep clear of business. Most of them sat silent, trying to translate *The Times* leading article, and glared every now and again at the two talkative ladies.

I exclude, also, breakfast in the air, which is not normally a happy occasion. Sleeping next to a stranger (unless the stranger has been especially selected for that purpose) can be an embarrassment anywhere. In the cramped quarters of an aeroplane it's dreadful. And after a disturbed and neck-stiffening night, internally disordered, unshaven and dishevelled, pecking morosely at pre-cooked, gym-shoe-textured omelette, I feel I should not be expected to speak to anyone about anything, let alone listen to the fidgety 18-stone raconteur who invariably turns up in the seat next to mine. But even if you have your closest business associates alongside, the tail-end of an east-bound transatlantic journey is not an occasion upon which to talk business.

When I was a young man, I used to be invited from time to time to spend the weekend with people who breakfasted in style. There was invariably a huge hot-plate on the sideboard, stocked with bloaters, kidneys, eggs and bacon, coffee, Indian tea and lapsang souchong, Jersey or Guernsey milk, shredded wheat, stewed fruit, cold ham, and two ironed copies of *The Financial Times*. I am proud to say that I still know a few such people. But none of them ever comes down to breakfast.

The Chief Steward in the *Queen Mary* told me once that on her pre-war voyages the 1st-class dining-room was always full for breakfast, and he used to stock twenty-two brands of marmalade. When the new cruise-ship *Cunard Adventurer* was put on the drawing-board, thirty years later, it was correctly assumed that the majority of her passengers were unaccustomed to eating eggs and bacon in public and would just want Continental breakfast in their cabins.

I think that a statue should be erected to the man who invented breakfast in bed. Even if your waistline limits you to half-a-cup of China tea and a Bath Oliver biscuit, it's still a civilised meal, particularly on a Sunday. You can smarten up your morale to face the day. You can once again determine not to drink so much brandy late at night. You can go over your plans for the Board Meeting. You can rehearse that impromptu speech. You can, in short, do a lot of important business over breakfast in bed, as Winston Churchill's colleagues found to their cost.

After the Prince Consort contretemps in Dallas, I vowed I would never attend another working breakfast as long as I lived. Some years later, however, the Mayor of Long Beach, California, sent me a cable at Cunard in London, asking me to meet him for breakfast in New York on the following day, to discuss an important new project. Courtesy (I thought) demanded that, on this occasion, I break my vow as well as my fast. My colleagues and I duly presented ourselves to His Worship at the appointed hour and place.

It was just as well that we did, because by the end of breakfast we had succeeded in selling him the *Queen Mary*.

# 6

# A three-line whip

ON FRIDAY 10 July, a dreadful thing happened to me. I opened my post and found that I had been sent a three-line Whip. I was bewildered and hurt. I have been a member of the House of Lords for over thirty years, and nobody has ever done such a thing to me before. Two lines, well, so be it. But three! What next?

It has now become clear what's next, and very disturbing it is, too. Owing to the creation of a large number of Life Peers the normal attendance in the Lords has been steadily and significantly increasing. We have had to put a lot more armchairs in the library, and the list of speakers for debates has become so lengthy that you can no longer get up after tea and begin your speech with those poignant words, "My Lords, at this late hour . . ."

This also means that at any moment the Government may be faced with a snap division, and if we get caught out and lose an important amendment, or worse still the Second Reading of a Bill, we're not going to endear ourselves to our colleagues in the Commons, and the next round of talks about Lords Reform will begin on quite a sour note.

Some members feel that we have now lost one of the great advantages that a Peer possesses, namely, the right to tell the

Chief Whip what he can do with it.

The other advantages of being a Peer are of course pretty generally recognised. The House of Lords is the finest Club in the world: its demeanour is civilised and urbane, the Club premises are good, the rules are sensible, and the service superb. Disraeli once remarked that the House of Lords reminded him of a ducal residence with his Grace lying dead in an upper chamber, but although the Lords is hardly the place to go for kicks, Dizzy was, I think, exaggerating. And there's no denying that there's less chance of having a C.S. gas-bomb lobbed at you in the Lords than there is down the Corridor in the Commons.

A title also helps you to get tickets for the theatre, or a table at the Savoy, but you have to tip disproportionately well in return. And at the rate of redemption current in most West End cloakrooms my umbrellas must now cost me about £25 each. Bankers and tailors are also beguiled by a title, but your overdraft and your overcoat will probably cost you more. And when the Playboy Club opened up in Park Lane, nearly every Peer of my acquaintance was invited to apply for membership, not to mention my Uncle Hubert who's been dead for many years.

A title is, however, a mixed blessing when travelling abroad. Some foreign porters and taxi-drivers seem to be impressed. Americans, on the other hand, probably because their jazz musicians tend to have names like Count Basie, Earl Hines and Duke Ellington, are understandably puzzled.

I was once invited to address the Alabama branch of the English Speaking Union on the role of the House of Lords in our Constitution. I touched lightly on Magna Carta and the Petition of Rights. I explained in greater detail the relationship between the Executive and the Legislature, and drew a nice distinction between a Private Bill and a Private Member's Bill. I performed the same service for the Lord Chamberlain and the Lord Great Chamberlain. I also, I'm ashamed to say, indulged in flippancy at the expense of the Judicial Committee of the

Privy Council.

I was listened to in stunned silence, and this continued well into question time. Eventually, to ease the embarrassment, the caretaker of the hall rose helpfully to his feet. "Why," he asked, "is the daughter-in-law of a dook called Lady George Whatsit? She ain't a fella, is she?" You can't really blame the Americans for being confused, and it is as well therefore to be in a position to explain, among other things, why Miss Raine McCorquodale, Mrs. Gerald Legge, Viscountess Lewisham, and the Countess of Dartmouth have all been the same pretty person.

In Japan it's worse. What's more, the Japs used to have titles themselves, and therefore ought to know better. "You have a reservation for me?" I inquired at my Tokyo hotel, "Lord Mancroft?" "Ah, yes, Mr. Lord," they replied, bowing low, "one moment, please." "No, no," I said, seeing disaster looming, "Lord is not my name, it's only a title—but it really doesn't matter. Not to worry at all." "Ah, yes, Mr. Title," they said, beaming, happily, "we understand of course. So sorry. This way, please."

In some countries, therefore, titled travellers might be well advised to abandon their titles temporarily, and adopt a nom de voyage. Even so, they should always remember to ask for letters under the names of Mr. Lord, Mr. Bart, Mr. Rev, and Mr. Esq, as well as under their own.

These, however, are only minor disadvantages, and happily for some the major disadvantage of having a peerage has now been done away with. Until recently you could not sit in the Commons if you had become a Lord, or sit in the Lords if you were born a Lady. Both these biological handicaps have now been put to rights, and the repercussions have been less convulsive than was feared. There remains, then, the problem of the three-line Whip.

Shortly after I had signed the Roll, and taken my seat for the first time in the Lords, the division bells began to ring. I thought it would be a good idea to find out what we were supposed to be voting for. (I naturally had all that sort of nonsense knocked out of me as soon as I was appointed a Junior Minister.) So I went up timidly to a character of majestic mien who was standing by the fireplace (I took him to be one of our Nobler Dukes, or at least a Scottish Representative Peer). "Sir," I said, "may I inquire what we are voting for?" "My Lord," he replied, "I am only the chap who fills up the coal scuttles. But since you've been good enough to ask my advice, let me give it to you. Never ask what you're voting for. Ask *whom* you're voting against."

That, I believe, is the nicest thing about being a Peer. In the long run you're beholden to nothing but your own conscience, though it is, of course, inadvisable to go for a long run too often.

As well as being the best Club, the House of Lords is also the finest Senate in the world. I am very proud to be a member of it, and I would not wish it otherwise. It can throw up an expert on every imaginable subject who only talks if he or she has something useful to say. We can debate wide-ranging subjects for which the Commons can't find immediate time.

The debates are good, though not always quite as good as we like to tell ourselves they are. This is not the only reason they are ill-reported in the press, but rather because public interest is and must be in the Commons. Politics is about Power, and it is in the Commons that Power lies.

We can revise untidy legislation and initiate our own. We can ultimately put a brake on dictatorship. But none of this can dispel a sense of frustration and impotence, or counteract the feeling of political make-believe that has been at the back of most attempts at Lords Reform.

Now, accidentally, the three-line Whip brings new life to the Lords. We may even start to matter. Whether this will prove an advantage remains to be seen. It will be seen by the first Noble and Tory Lord who lingers too long over the Cockburn '27, and, finding himself locked out of the Lobby, accidentally brings down the Government.

Sheridan's friend, Lord Bayforth, refused to leave White's for a Motion standing in his own name on the Order Paper until he had finished his second bottle of port, and the Lords waited patiently for him. When he did eventually turn up I'm sorry to say he was drunk.

The Lords, of course, have now changed in this respect as in others, though nobody has ever seemed quite clear whether the expression "Drunk as a Lord" should be taken as a compliment, or an insult.

# 7

# My next yacht

MY NEXT yacht is going to be much bigger than my last. Actually there was some doubt in the upper echelons of the Bembridge Sailing Club as to whether a scruffy secondhand dinghy named *The Crab* ought to have been classed as a yacht at all.

In other respects, too, her debut had been inauspicious. The very day we acquired her she slipped her moorings, and, without any help from us, ran away to sea. The Coastguards apprehended her in the nick of time, and this was just as well because when Harry Hulbert's boat broke loose the previous week it ended up on the beach at Ostend, and Harry had to apply for an import licence to get her back. It was apparently thought that her return unlicensed might have prejudiced the British boat-building industry.

A contrite *Crab* was duly restored to us. We loaded her with thermos flasks, Norwich terriers, and other essential gear, and set course for Itchenor. Five minutes and two cable lengths later we rammed Lord Brabazon full amidships in *Tara*, and this was an encounter which not even the *Queen Mary* would have undertaken with impunity.

Lord B. of T. was very nice about it. Well, fairly nice. It was generally understood, he reminded us, that the two most useless things in a small boat were an umbrella and a Naval Officer. But now (looking pointedly at me) he had a third candidate to put forward. And in any case, what was that I had on my head?

He was referring, I supposed, to my new green woollen pom-pom hat. I had bought it specially for the Bembridge Regatta, which is always a very pukka affair. Rear-Commodores and others stride around wearing white-topped caps and purposeful expressions. To appear amongst them bare-headed would, I felt, be inadequate, and to wear a white-topped cap would have been above my station. I suspected, however, that I must have misjudged the situation when the Bembridge policeman came into the Club and complained that the entrance was being blocked by a Rover car owned by a gentleman wearing a green woollen pom-pom hat. Clifton, our steward, replied sharply that no gentleman would ever wear a green woollen pom-pom hat. Apart from this the Bembridge folk were extremely kind, and I enjoyed my membership of their Club. Indeed, I find that my banker's order is still in existence even though I left the Island many years ago.

I'm afraid, however, that I cannot agree with Ratty that there is nothing, absolutely nothing, better than simply messing about in boats. There is. Yachts, for instance—great big 100-footers, with six double bedrooms and colour TV. I could mess about in them for ever.

Of course there is a wide range of alternatives between *The Crab* and a 100-footer, and I have considered them all.

We don't want to get involved in anything like hard work; no blistered palms; no salt spray whipping through the hair, or any nonsense like that. Mr. Heath has not actually invited me to join the crew of his *Morning Cloud*, but if he were to do so I should have to decline. I am, however, comforted to read that you can disregard any of his orders as long as you say "Sir" at the end of your speech of resignation.

I have always thought that to own a racing yacht would be tantamount to tearing up five pound notes under a cold shower. Mr. Heath however is reported to have described *Morning*

*Cloud* as a "bloody good investment". If so, it must be the first yacht to qualify as an investment since Noah built the *Ark*.

No round-the-world single-handed stuff, either. I am enchanted with my own company, but not when I'm being seasick.

A three-ton cabin cruiser? How many does that sleep in comfort? None. And what happens if you're cooped up with a lot of dear friends whom you find you loathe and you aren't due back until Wednesday week?

This happened once to the late and sadly missed Lord Stanley of Alderley. He signed on an earnest young Welsh engineer as a deck-hand. Unhappily they fell out, and Ed Stanley berated him so soundly that the poor fellow threatened to put the matter into the hands of his solicitor as soon as they made Cornwall. "You may," said Ed calmly "put the matter into the hands of your solicitor, or into any other portion of his anatomy which your ingenuity or his forbearance will permit." As soon, however, as they had tied up at Pendragon Creek the young man rushed to the phone box to tell his lawyer what had happened. With such Celtic volubility was he doing this that he failed to notice Ed creeping up behind him with a tool kit, and screwing him into the phone box. The boy was soon released because he had only to dial 999, or whatever it is you dial when an eccentric Peer of the Realm has immured you in a Cornish phone box. But the episode caused comment round Pendragon for quite some time to come.

So nothing cribbed, cabinned and confined for me. I shall acquire a yacht that'll make that little job of A. Onassis look like a Connemara coracle.

I shan't worry about the cost, because Mr. J. Pierpont Morgan tells me that if I have to worry about the cost of a yacht I obviously can't afford one. I shan't, of course, be paying British taxes, because I shall be permanently tied up in Portofino or Antibes. This, after all, is the principal reason for owning a yacht. I have never heard of anybody owning a 100-footer that regularly put to sea.

The Hohenzollerns and the Hapsburgs did not own yachts in order to go anywhere. They merely wanted to wipe the eye of the Czar, the Khedive, and King Edward VII.

I shall lack for nothing. Henri Sartori will be my private chef. The Amadeus String Quartet will play Mozart on the poop-deck. There will be lashings of caviare, and Charles Heidsieck Blanc de Blancs, and I must remember to find out what is the decimalised version of a lashing in case anything runs out. The Misses Taylor, Loren, Bardot, Lollobrigida, Ege and Welch will be my constant guests, and *The Financial Times* will arrive by air each morning. Bliss.

On second thoughts I shall have to put to sea once a year in order to avoid getting stuck for the local rates. I shall, of course, fly a flag of convenience so that I can't be held responsible if I get the charts upside down, and collide with somebody in the Channel. Whither shall I sail? Why, Bembridge, of course, though I shan't be able to get into the Harbour. Thanks to British Rail this is now silting up. I shall therefore have no problem with British yacht tonnage. This is calculated on the amount of square foot of deck open to the sun, and you have to pay about £1 a ton every time you enter a harbour.

It's a very complicated calculation. One of the chaps at the Admiralty whose job it was to do it eventually went mad and designed a yacht of such extraordinary proportions that its tonnage worked out at minus seven. He then sailed it all round Britain demanding £7 off the harbour-master at every port of call.

I shall hope to arrive off Bembridge in time for their annual Regatta, where the presence of my yacht may help to discountenance their uppity neighbours at Cowes. I shall, of course, say nothing about that banker's order. I shall just stand on the bridge, and touch my hat cordially to all my old friends as they sail past. And the hat, I need hardly add, will be green, woollen, and pom-pommed.

# 8

# A few light snacks

WHEN BOSWELL and Johnson were visiting the Isle of Mull, their hostess, Lady Lochsay, offered them cold sheep's head for breakfast. At the thought of this delicacy, even the Doctor's formidable gorge rose in revolt, and he waxed indignant about the incident in his *Journal*. So, more quietly, did Boswell in his.

Both works carried such detailed descriptions of what the two friends ate and drank that Mrs. Thrale brought it upon herself to reprove them. It was not nice, she told them firmly, for a gentleman to show so much care for his sustenance. Johnson replied sharply that if a man didn't care for his belly he would care for nothing.

I daren't think what Mrs. Thrale would have to say on this subject if she were alive today. There's more written now about food and drink than about anything else except sex and race relations. Pretty well every newspaper and magazine has its regular wine correspondent. Even our local paper in Gloucestershire has entered the lists. Last month's County wine-making contest, for instance, attracted serious attention. Winners in the home-made claret section were Mrs. X (fruity, well-rounded), Mrs. Y (fine colour and full-bodied), and Miss Z (slightly acid, but should improve if laid down).

In wider journalistic fields all tastes are catered for, from admirers of the 1924 Mouton Rothschild to devotees of Château Plonque. In *The Financial Times* Edmund Penning-Rowsell deploys an expertise in keeping with the rest of the paper. Andrew Graham has, alas, been forced by illness to leave *The Times*, where his scholarly and gentle notes are much missed. Pamela Vandyke Price has taken his place. She appears to enjoy controversy, but even so, she mustn't encourage us to drink whisky with oysters. Cyril Ray in *The Director* wanders entertainingly off the beaten track, particularly in Italy and Central Europe. He even finds nice things to say about Cyprus sherry, but he is not well-briefed about borage. In *Harpers & Queen* Humphrey Lyttleton is practical, critical and very funny. He rightly deserved to win a Glenfiddick Prize as the wine-and-food writer of the year. (But as I was one of the judges I am naturally biased.)

There are now dozens of expert wine writers to suit all tastes and every prejudice. A particular prejudice of my own is a distrust of over-decorative writing. Even the magisterial André Simon could not always resist temptation, and when he spoke rapturously of a full body, a delicate nose, and a prospect of well-developed ripeness, one might be forgiven for asking whether he was discussing Brigitte Bardot or the Vosne-Romanée, La Grande Rue, 1949.

James Thurber did much to sober us up when he offered a naïve little native Burgundy, and hoped that we would be "amused by its presumption". And Stephen Potter, with tongue still further in cheek, spoke of "the imperial decay of his invalid port, its gracious withdrawal from perfection keeping a hint of former majesty withal as it hovered between oblivion and the divine *untergang* of infinite recession". The circle of wine writers under the Chairmanship of Sir Trevor Lloyd-Hughes, K.B., M.A., rightly disapproves of such flourishes, but not, I suspect, without a wistful sigh of regret.

Making speeches about wine requires even more control than writing about it. I have been asked to do so only once, and I failed with ignominy. Together with Sir David Webster (the late Director-General of Covent Garden Opera) I was to be installed as a Commandeur du Tastevin in Burgundy. The ceremony began at 6.30 p.m., when 600 of us sat down to dinner in the caves of the Clos de Vougeot. Seven wines and five hours later, I was suddenly, and without warning, called upon to make a speech in French. Not only was I by then unable to utter a single word of French—I could say very little in English either. Indeed, I could hardly stagger to my feet.

It was just as well that we had taken the precaution of bringing our chauffeur with us. Unfortunately, however, he had forgotten the name of the hotel in Dijon where we lodged. So, at about two o'clock in the morning we were to be found circulating between the Toison d'Or, the Chapeau Rouge and the Central Hotel, where puzzled night porters were asked if they could lay any claim to the somnolent Commandeurs in the back.

To all those who write about wine, let alone speak about it, I raise my glass. Thanks to their work, many of us have acquired increasing knowledge and appreciation of one of the delights that distinguish the Barbarian from the civilised man. I envy their enthusiasm and expertise. I am glad, too, that they are now writing for the man of humble means and humbler cellar space, rather than just for the millionaire.

They have, of course, in this country, an advantage over their foreign brethren, because, with all respect to General Sir Guy Salisbury Jones, the doyen of British wine-growers, we grow no great wine here ourselves. Try asking for claret in Cologne, or Mosel in Marseilles, and you'll see the advantage this gives not only to the British wine-bibber, but to his advisers, too. The British writer has a wider vineyard in which to range, and many more grapes from which to choose.

I was put in mind of this the other day when I was looking through my Guzzle Book. This is my own modest and rather disreputable contribution to the literature of wine and food. In it I've noted down over the years meals I have particularly enjoyed, and wines which I wished to remember. There is a number for the food, a letter for the wine, an asterisk for the ambience, and a nominal roll of the company present.

During a particularly uncomfortable period of the war, when my Regiment was replete with Spam and biscuits, some of us who had travelled together in happier times used to compose meals from memory, just to cheer ourselves up. I would start with the main course—say 27F. (This had been enjoyed at M. Thulier's Oustau de Baumanière near Les Baux-de-Provence: a superb Gigot d'Agneau en Croûte helped down with a new Gigondas.) "Well," responded my Battery Captain, "we shall want something pretty light before that, shan't we? What about 18K?" "Agreed." (This was a brook trout lately swimming in its tank outside the Goldener Hirsch at Neuenahr, and escorted by a mouthful of Piesporter Michelsberg. Nice stuff.)

One item in the book which recently caught my eye had, however, slipped my memory. 117K. Against it I had put both a question and an exclamation mark. I rang up the particular friend with whom I had shared that luncheon.

"Donald," I said, "117K." "Of course," he replied. "The New Inn at Coln St. Aldwyns."

"But why the exclamation mark, and why the query? What was it about that lunch that both aroused our excitement and raised questions in our minds? Was it the Lafite '53, or the wonderful steak-and-kidney pudding, with mushroom sauce, tender spring greens and dear little new potatoes?"

"Don't be daft," my friend replied, "it was nothing to do with the meal at all. It was the waitress."

One day I may come across a man who has married a girl for her knowledge of claret. That'll be a turn-up for the book.

# 9

# The City by night

MY MOTHER once had a loin of pork lobbed into her lap as she was driving back from a dance to her home in the Charterhouse. This *must* have been an accident. The Smithfield meat porters knew her well by sight and this was hardly surprising because she was a very pretty girl and in those days there weren't many pretty girls living in the heart of the City. And, come to think of it, I don't suppose there can be many more living there today.

There are of course two cities of London. There's the City of the day—the Square Mile teeming with a financial expertise and an integrity that is the envy of all beholders but a city which can occasionally drop a few interesting bricks. Then comes the evening and the markets are hushed. The paper darts are garnered from the floor of the Stock Exchange and gnarled night watchmen begin to thump around Lloyds and the Baltic. The Bears, the Bulls, the Stags and a million other sharp-witted animals get their bowler-hatted heads down for the 6.21 to Rickmansworth.

After that you can see the City of the night and a very odd place it is too. It's a City of lonely policemen, of cleaners, cats and fish-porters. It's a place of empty streets, deserted pubs and of sudden, surprisingly beautiful vistas. The spire of St. Bride's (the Madrigal in Stone) looks even more delicious at midnight against a full August moon than it does when you're stuck beneath it in a traffic block on your way to an urgent noon-time appointment. "Not to worry," said my taxi driver consolingly. "Defence of the Realm comes into all this. If the Russians landed tomorrow, I reckon they'd get no further than Ludgate Hill."

So be it, but I find the City of the night more fascinating than the day. When my grandfather was resident physician to the Old Brothers of the Charterhouse, scarcely more than 10,000 people lived in the City. He worshipped in St. Bartholomew the Great, which was the only Norman church to resist both the Fire of 1666 and Hitler. In Victorian days, however, it was in a sad state of disrepair. The roof leaked, so the Rector, Sir Borrodaile Savory, had to hold up an umbrella whilst he was preaching, and his sermons were inclined to harp upon Noah, floods, and the waters of Babylon. The churchwardens eventually took the hint and sent for a tiler.

The City churches are fuller now than they were in my mother's day because they are open during the lunch hour for the benefit of a gratifyingly large number of City workers. But by night the City looks as desolate as it did fifty years ago, though my stockbroker tells me there's a restaurant which actually deploys belly dancers. Montagu Norman and my grandfather must be turning in their graves.

For some people the quiet can be overpowering. Between the wars Bombadier Bean in my regiment took a job as a caretaker with one of the City companies. He was a convivial fellow, born in Birmingham's Bull Ring and he liked noise. The utter silence of the City after dark got so much on his nerves that he eventually went mad. Bonkers. Right off his chump. They took him along to all the best chump doctors in Harley Street but to no avail. Then somebody had the bright idea of sending him back to stay with his Auntie May who earned her living as a cleaner at New Street Station in Birmingham. She lived in a small box over No. 7 platform and the racket was appalling, but it did the trick. In a few weeks the old boy was back in the City of London and as right as rain.

Incidentally, I believe the Lord Mayor is dining with another of the great City companies, the Worshipful Company of Balloonblowers, this very evening, and the thought of this makes me revise my theory of the two Cities. There are, of course, actually three—day, night, and this, the City of civic, gastronomic and oratorial twilight. A Lord Mayor of London has to make about 1,000 speeches a year, though some Lord Mayors have compromised by making the same speech 1,000 times. In the course of these endeavours the Lord Mayor will also have to eat in public about five hundred times and unless he has a stomach like the *QE2*'s boilers this will probably damage him for life. If it doesn't, then having to listen to about 4,000 speeches from other people undoubtedly will.

But oddly enough, London is not all that full of dying Lord Mayors, ailing Aldermen and broken-down Masters of City Companies. This is a tribute to their own ambition and stamina as well as to the remarkable skill of Messrs. Ring & Brymer, the caterers who for about three hundred years have nourished City functions out of hay-boxes, billy cans and Aldershot ovens slung together in Cannon Street, since few of the City halls seem to have any kitchens.

It's easy of course to laugh at the pomp of the Lord Mayoralty and poke fun at the circumstance of civic fol-de-rol. I don't. Napoleon maintained that as long as he had enough red and blue silk ribbon, he would never lack brave generals.

All right. Too few Masters of the Worshipful Company of Balloonblowers have anything to do with balloons? They only got into the act because their wives liked the idea of a knighthood? Too few Lord Mayors come from the leading City institutions? Too many have only been ambitious estate agents commuting from Pinner who liked the idea of a baronetcy even though they now have to settle for a GCMG?

Possibly. But the City of London is governed more efficiently and more honestly than any other capital in the world. And by and large it's these Balloonblowers who do it and though their wives may from time to time give them a meaningful nudge, most of them really do have the interests of the City at heart and are proud of its history, lavish in their charity and jealous of the City's customs and traditions.

And talk about hospitable! To be entertained by the Lord Mayor of London is still a privilege which the visitor rightly covets, be he Duke or Dustman. I remember being bidden by my friend, Sir Cullum Welch, when he was Lord Mayor, to a party in honour of some visiting potentates from Polynesia. Sir Cullum, hospitable fellow that he is, did them proud—State Trumpeters, Daimler Hire, flood-lighting, Moët et Chandon, and a veritable cornucopia of civic oratory, spilling far into the night. Many of the guests spoke only a delightful pidgin English and in due course their comments in this tongue came back. "Much meat," they reported. "Wine him bubble. Bugle him tootle. Big fella Cullum, him quack, quack. Big fella ten time him quack, quack. Plenty candle, plenty ricksha. Him sleepy time juju."

And talking of juju, what about the City's politics? Conservative of course, but not always as conservative as Central Office would like. The City used to be a separate constituency of its own but the Socialists put a stop to all that and made the City muck in with the neighbours down the road. The last City member was Sir Harold Webbe and I remember once taking a meeting for him when he lay sick of the palsy. It was a lunch-time meeting, of course. In the City politics die after dark, but at lunchtime they can be lively. My meeting was noisy by the City's refined standards, but when I had finished, the loudest heckler came up and to my astonishment told me that I had converted him. Furthermore, as a proof of his sincerity, he would like to join the Conservative Party. What was the smallest sum he would have to pay to join the Party? A shilling. He gave me a shilling and I gave him a receipt. I shook hands with him. The chairman shook hands with him. We were all photographed shaking hands with each other. I took him along to the "Green Man", hard by the Mansion House and bought him a double whisky. I gave him a brief resumé of our Party's manifesto and bought him another double whisky. I then rang up Harold Webbe and told him what had happened. "Good heavens," he said, "don't tell me that fellow's caught you too. He must have had more double whiskies for a shilling than any other man in London."

A tribute to the financial enterprise of the City if not to its integrity. But that was at lunchtime. You couldn't get away with that sort of thing after dark. Neither the Lord Mayor, nor the Sheriffs, nor the Master, nor even the Wardens would put up with it for a moment. Domine (as the City's motto goes) dirige nos.

# 10

# If only . . .

IF ONLY Mr. Moyses Stevens, the florist, hadn't suffered a momentary lapse of memory, my Uncle Harry wouldn't have been able to leave me a pipe of the Cockburn 1912 in his Will. What happened was this.

Uncle Harry was a great man for sending people flowers. People (particularly young female people) liked this, and they also liked the fact that his bouquet was always accompanied by a little card carrying an appropriate message written in his own fair hand. No typed cards or florists' handwriting for Uncle Harry! What people didn't know was that he kept an assorted stock of pre-written cards with Mr. Moyses Stevens. One, for instance, said simply "Hurrah!" This did well enough for births, marriages, engagements, and the advent of unexpected legacies, whilst another, saying, "I am so *deeply* distressed" came in handy for deaths, divorces, and legacies that failed.

One evening Uncle Harry was dining with the parents of a little red-headed piece named Maisie, upon whom he had designs. Unfortunately, whilst waving an arm to emphasise a nicely worded point, he inadvertently bowled a sauce-boat into the lap of Maisie's mother. His hostess was a mite disenchanted about this, so next morning Uncle Harry ordered a handsome bouquet to be dispatched. Unfortunately Mr. Moyses Stevens, instead of pinning on the deeply distressed card, accidentally sent the one which read, "What a wonderful evening! When can we do it again?" Poor Uncle was immediately banished from copper-nob's company, and what might have turned into a lasting romance was brought to a peremptory halt. Uncle Harry, as a matter of fact, never married at all, and eventually spent what spare shillings he could muster in collecting Piranesi prints and vintage port, and this, if only Mr. Stevens had been more thoughtful, might never have come my way.

With the possible exception of "Time, gentlemen, please," I regard the words "What might have been" as the saddest in the English language. They probably sound nearly as dispiriting in Urdu, Swahili, and Malay, and I know for certain that they do in German. When I was a student at Bonn University there used to hang in the English library a framed quotation from the poet Heine with a helpful translation underneath, "Opportunity may only knock at your door once in a lifetime. Grasp it: it may never return." Some savant had crossed out the word "lifetime" and substituted "nightdress"—but the sentiment remained a noble one.

Noble, but debatable. Some missed opportunities may eventually prove to be blessings in disguise. Uncle Harry used to tell me that one of the minor pleasures of middle age was looking back at the girls he hadn't married. And who knows whether Maisie might not have turned out a real vixen, and nagged the poor old boy into an early grave? We tend to put all our mistakes into a heap and call them our misfortunes. I suspect that "what might have been" might as often as not accrue to our distress. Do we not only remember the lost opportunities from which we might have profited, and conveniently forget the ones that would inevitably have landed us in the mud? That's the trouble with ifonliness.

If only I'd marked Leeds United to win at home last Saturday I might well be dining off pâté de foie gras to the sound of trumpets for the rest of my life. If only I'd bought Better Mousetraps instead of switching into IOS I might now be nuzzling some blonde on the deck of my yacht at Antibes. That's all very well, but you forget that if you hadn't marked Norwich City to draw, and if you hadn't picked up Cunard when they were only eleven bob, you might well now be in the poor house.

Even the shrewd Israelis are not proof against this confusion of thought. They mutter, for instance, and shake their heads whenever the name of Moses is mentioned. If you ask them why this should be they reply, "Well, think. If only the old gentleman had turned right instead of left when he brought the Children of Israel out of the Wilderness, we might now have oil instead of all these confounded oranges."

Well, that's as maybe; and whilst we are out in Mesopotamia what about the Garden of Eden? If only Eve had done what she was told, and left that wretched apple untasted, we might all be better situated than we are today. But you can't bet on it. I've always regarded poor Eve as a bit of a rattle-brain, and if the author of Genesis c.3 has got his facts right she was also very short of tact. So even if she had managed to pull herself together and send the serpent about his business, she would probably have dug another heffalump trap for herself in a couple of days, and done something equally chuckle-headed. Then we'd all be in the same old mess as before.

By and large, History comes down firmly against the wisdom of moaning about what might have been. If only, for instance, Guy Fawkes had actually succeeded in blowing up the House of Commons, do you really think we should have been saved from Oliver Cromwell? I doubt it. And if only Christopher Columbus had listened to his crew, and turned back when their courage failed them, would America have remained undiscovered for long? Of course not. In next to no time some other Nosey Parker would have cast off for Atlantis, or El Dorado, or whatever it was they were all looking for, only to bump eventually into Boston by mistake.

And now Lord Harvey of Tashurst's Diplomatic Diaries have set the pundits by the ears. If only the Generals' Assassination putsch had not so narrowly failed and if only we had called Hitler's bluff at the time of Munich, could we not have prevented World War II? And has anybody explained what would have happened if only Hitler had declared war on Japan at the time of Pearl Harbour, and thus aligned himself with America? Would America have rejected Germany's advances? But the piece of history that really worries me is this. What would have happened if only Pontius Pilate had not changed his mind about Barabbas?

But all this is a little above our station. For us ordinary mortals, it's the pillow-biter by which we judge the importance of what might have been. You know, of course, what a pillow-biter is? You wake up in the middle of the night, and you break into a muck sweat as memories come flooding back of some ghastly brick that you once dropped, or some unpardonable solecism you long ago committed. So you bite your pillow in an agony of remorse. "If only I had not drunk so much at the Wotherspoon wedding, and thrown my arms so effusively around the Archdeacon's neck as my wife was anxiously wheeling me home, might I not now be Chairman of the Rural District Council?" "If only I had not put all those white mice in the Science Master's shirt drawer, might I not have won that splendid scholarship to Wolverhampton Tech.?"

My own worst pillow-biter was conceived in the officers' ward room of the SS *William H. Daniels* on 5 June 1944. We were at the time lying off Southend, waiting to proceed next day to the beaches of Normandy in the normal course of business. About seven hundred of us had been living for nearly a week in exhilarating discomfort on the open deck of this scruffy but hospitable little petrol coaster. Her officers were the soul of kindness, and they unselfishly let about forty of us eat in rotation in their miniscule Mess. As I waited my turn for a place at the table I was gazing out of the port-hole towards Southend, a view which we had been admiring for several days and of which we were by that time heartily sick. "Heavens above," I exclaimed in exasperation, "how much longer are we going to be kept hanging about here?" I was referring, of course, to Southend, but the poor little Chief Engineer, snatching a hurried meal of beans and bacon at his own table, obviously thought I was complaining about the length of time I had been kept waiting for luncheon. "I've been eating as fast as I can" he muttered, and left the room.

If only I had realised in time how horrifyingly I had been misunderstood. But it was too late. I never saw him again to apologise, and I still bite my pillow in recollection of this enormity. If only he reads this, I may be able to put the matter to rights; if only this catches his eye I shall invite him, by way of atonement, to help me polish off Uncle Harry's port.

# 11

# Off the Tourist track

OUR NEIGHBOURS from down the road asked if they could come in and show us their holiday snaps. We said, "Yes, of course," but we said it with a slightly guilty conscience because we hadn't even noticed that they'd been away. Where had they been? Well, round the world actually. Was that nice? Well, yes, it was, but the trouble is it's going to be so difficult to find somewhere new to go next year.

I sympathise. When I was a child my sisters and I were sent to Cromer for our hols, and if you study the map carefully you will realise that there is nothing between Cromer and the North Pole. I don't know whether our parents sent us there to enjoy ourselves, or simply to toughen us up. But I can say in all honesty that nothing I subsequently endured at my public school, or on the beaches of Normandy, was anything like as purifying as Cromer sands on an ordinary English summer day.

That, of course, was fifty years ago, and since then the whole world of tourism and travel has undergone a revolution. St. Augustine said, "The whole world is a book, and those who do not travel read only one page." Quite so, but not even St. Augustine could have envisaged that sixteen centuries later more money was going to be spent on travel between countries than on any other single commodity in world trade. And that's a lot of pages to read.

Two hundred years ago, only the English milord and his son could afford the Grand Tour. Today the package tour and the group affinity air fare have put the whole world in everybody's pocket. When a fortnight's holiday to California costs as little as £135 it's not surprising that everyone's been everywhere, and is now busily looking for somewhere else to go.

The travel brochures emphasise the difficulty. "People in search of peace and quiet," says a Swiss publication I've just received, "are flocking to Lake San Profito from all over the world." In next to no time, of course, the flockers will be complaining that the place has been ruined by tourists. They overlook the fact that they themselves have probably contributed to the ruin. A few of the natives may have different views. No doubt they dislike being jostled off their streets and crowded out of the shops, but maybe they also appreciate the improved drainage system, and take a good view of the hospital extension, the newly planted trees and widened roads; and they suspect that tourism may possibly have contributed to these blessings. They may even remember how the poet sang

> The Swiss, a careful, prudent breed,
> Foresee the tourist's slightest need,
> And thank Horizon, Cooks and Poly
> For bring in the English lolly.

Other countries go to greater lengths to inject elements of novelty into the jaded tourist routine. "Are you seeking thrills and adventures in a strange land?" asks an advertisement in a Detroit newspaper. "Join the US Information Service as a combat librarian." (I suspect, however, that it will be some time before any British tour operator organises package tours to Vietnam.)

For the genuine seeker after something different, new vistas are opening up daily. Deep-sea fishing and big game photography are now within the reach of all, and often acceptably far from the beaten track. "Wasn't this once cannibal country?" asked an anxious American matron as she prepared to go on a Central African safari. "Why, yes, indeed," replied her guide reassuringly, "but that was many years ago. You have nothing, Madam, to fear today. Though I may add that if by any sad mischance an accident were to overtake you, you wouldn't actually be wasted."

I wonder if the travel wheel may not eventually turn full cycle, and if the best place for us to take a new and unfamiliar holiday may not be found much nearer home. The overcrowded tourist circuit of Oxford, Stratford, Windsor and Winchester is to be avoided. There is still, however, a great deal of our beautiful country that is unknown and still unspoilt. St. Paul's and the Abbey are now so jammed with tourists that we may forget they were originally built for divine worship, and not for choc-ices and polaroid cameras. England, however, is full of splendid cathedrals and churches, many of which have hardly ever seen a tourist.

So before you pack your bags for Acapulco, Ankor Wat, or Lake San Profito, why not take a look at some of the less well-known bits of Britain? Take Central Wales for instance. That's a wonderful bit of No-Tourists-land. You won't, at the time of going to press, find a Hilton or a Sheraton at Llandrindod Wells, but the little pubs and hotels of Wales have superb mutton, and give an excellent, if simple, service. A dead-pan report from the Welsh Tourist Board once described how a young (unmarried) couple sought to occupy the only bedroom in a tiny Snowdonian pub. The landlady wasn't so sure that they were really on their honeymoon, and she demanded to see their marriage lines. Of course, they had none, but they did have the wit to produce a driving licence. She was Welsh-speaking, and not really understanding the licence, was duly deceived. When her English-speaking husband returned he smelled a rat, and shouted anxiously through the key-hole, "If you haven't done it, don't do it—this isn't for it."

So when your friends proudly show you their snaps of Table

Mountain and Teheran, tell them about the Weald of Kent in spring and the Cotswolds, describe a market day in King's Lynn mention the plovers in South Uist, or Evensong in All Hallows-By-The-Tower. And if, as a last resort, you're seeking a really original holiday, why not just stay at home? Watch your family working in the garden. Explain to them that your role as a gardener corresponds to that of Queen Victoria as a Constitutional Monarch, namely to encourage, to warn, and to be consulted. Have an argument with the Vicar about the New English Bible. Read one of that impressive stack of ten-ton books on your coffee-table. Learn to play the lute. Covet your neighbour's wife. Take up petit-point. Write a novel, potter, or simply do nothing, and do it with charm and a clear conscience. That'll startle everybody, including yourself.

# 12

# The number-plate game

THE FIRST car in which I had any proprietary interest was a 1923 bull-nosed Morris-Cowley. It was painted red down one side and blue down the other to confuse witnesses in case of an accident.

No such anxieties seemed to inhibit Sir Gerald Nabarro, whose cars boldly bore registration plates numbered NAB 1, 2, 3 and so on. This practice is now widespread, and although it irritates some people it seems to me an innocent conceit. Surely the late Lord Brabazon of Tara, who held the first civil pilot's licence, had every reason to be proud of his FLY 1, which his 96-year-old widow still gamely sports? So also is the Marquis of Exeter, President since 1934 of the Amateur Athletics Association, proud of his AAA 1.

A 1 itself, of course, belongs to the Chairman of Lloyd's, and who could deny FIJ 1 to the Fijian High Commissioner? RAB 1, however, does not, as you might think, belong to the Master of Trinity College, Cambridge. It is (unless Lord Butler has recently done a deal) the property of a bookmaker.

All this reveals another side of the coin, and one which, I suspect, can cause difficulties. My daughters were at school with a pretty girl named Sally Lewis—Sarah Olwen Lewis, to set it out in full. On her 21st birthday her parents gave her a Mini, and also bought for her at considerable expense, the number SOL 21. Behind this insignia she trundles proudly round the town. She has now, however, become engaged to a Naval Officer named Westmacott, and not unnaturally she is having second thoughts about her number plate. A Mini SOW may give rise to comment.

This problem is not new. I first came across it when I was Parliamentary Under-Secretary at the Home Office, twenty years ago. The late Mr. S. O. Davies (then M.P. for Merthyr Tydfil) had been refused permission to use his own initials on his number plate, and a row was brewing. I was told to look into the matter, and I discovered, to my joy, that the Home Office kept a list of letters which were not allowed to appear in combination on any car number plate. My goodness, the things the Home Office had thought of! Some, of course, were predictable. Not even the trendiest of Bishops could be allowed to ride around in a car numbered GOD, nor DUW if his bishopric were in Wales. SEX wouldn't do at all, nor, for differing reasons, would WOP, WOG, or even JEW. One could also understand that HMG and HRH obviously had special uses. But many of the other combinations which the Home Office thought too rude for public gaze shed an interesting light on the workings of the official mind. Some you can guess for yourselves, but one combination (which I'm sorry to say I've forgotten) was not so straightforward. It turned out to be the Rumanian word for lesbian, and it was apparently thought unwise if it were to be accidentally displayed on the car of two school mistresses sightseeing in Bucharest. Very thorough, the Home Office!

All this, however, was twenty years ago. I expect that times have changed, and that nowadays almost anything goes on a car; no censorship of the bumper by permissive minds in the Home Office. One thing, however, I do know. Getting hold of the number you want is comparatively easy. Getting rid of one you don't want is quite a different matter. A friend of mine in the American Embassy has been allotted a number plate prefaced by the letters SOB. Since Americans are much more touchy about being called a son of a bitch than we are, he's trying to get rid of the thing as soon as possible. But he tells me it's proving an uphill struggle.

Actually, the car number conceit has never caught on in America, and this is odd because the Americans love personalisation even more than we do. They have monograms on their shirts and pyjamas, HIS and HERS on their bath towels, and their names and home towns inscribed on enormous lapel and bosom badges when they go down to Miami for the annual convention of the American Bee-keepers' Association. This badge habit has always had its critics in Britain, but it's very useful, though, of course, open to malpractice. At the last Conservative Conference one constituency treasurer went around wearing a lapel badge proclaiming himself to be Miss Diana Dors. It was three days before this was spotted. There was an indignant paragraph in his local paper but the reaction of Miss Dors was not recorded.

The reason why the Americans are not as interested in car personalisation as we are is simple. They change their cars and their number plates nearly every year, so a British-type operation would be a waste of effort. This, I think, is a pity, because I can see that an American official with a sense of occasion could have quite a lot of fun issuing number plates such as FDR, JFK, HST and LBJ to motorists of an inappropriate political complexion.

The Americans, accordingly, use their number plates for local propaganda rather than for personal advertisement. The cars of motorists from Florida proclaim that theirs is The Sunshine State, Kentucky is The Blue Grass State, Connecticut The Nutmeg State, and so on. How would we fare if we adopted the habit here? Well, Cornwall presumably would be The Riviera County, Devon would be Glorious, and Skegness So Bracing. But when you came to size up Wigan, or the Gorbals, you might find yourself in some difficulty.

In point of fact the Americans are not too keen for their cars to be readily recognisable by their neighbours or the police. They belong to the blue/red Morris-Cowley rather than to the NAB school of thought, though it would, of course, have been difficult to mistake Sir Gerald even if he were driving a hearse, or a stop-me-and-buy-one. On the same principle, though for different reasons, the Chairman of one much troubled public company never visits his works in his own car—he lets Hertz or Avis run the risk of reprisals.

Personalisation is not confined to persons. Government Departments, for instance, have always been lavish in their use of the Royal cipher. You will find it everywhere from Parliament to pillar-boxes. Before the War, the Cambridge Military Hospital at Aldershot used to stock "Domestic utensils rubber, lunatic officers for the use of", and there, opposite the handle, was the good old lion and unicorn. Thoughtful; but carrying things, I feel, a little bit too far.

That's nothing new, of course, in personalisation. When Sir Bertram de Beltuppe charged into battle with his fellow knights at Agincourt they were so covered in ironmongery that they couldn't tell friend from foe. They could hardly tack a number plate onto their palfrey's pastern, so they festooned themselves in lions rampant, stags couchant, and kippers flippant. Hence heraldry. France had Henri IV and François I, with their salamanders and porcupines, and there was always Napoleon with his bees. In our own time those dreadful swastikas and fasces were plastered over all Europe. Mussolini could at least plead a respectable precedent. Ancient Rome was decorated with the initials SPQR from humble drain covers and wine jars, to the standards of the Centurions and the rods of the lictors guarding the chariot of Caius Julius Caesar as he rode in triumph through the city. If you'd nipped between the lictors' legs, and round to the back of the chariot, you would probably have found a little plate proudly inscribed CJC I.

Incidentally, one of Caesar's Engineers was named Nerva Antoninus Balbus, and you can guess what the initials on *his* chariot plate would have been.

# 13

# Travelling carefully

THIS WAS their Captain speaking from the flight deck, and his voice was meaningful and leaderworthy. "Folks," he said, "I have two pieces of noos for you, one good and one bad. First the bad, We're lost. And now for the good, We're well ahead of Skedool." The air hostess reassumed her air hostess smile, and everybody relaxed. They had been taken into Capt. Bobbliwobski's confidence, and all was therefore well.

This, I feel, is the correct approach when things are going agley, and they are bound to go agley even more as travel becomes daily more precipitate and international travel regulations more enigmatic. I'm surprised that chaos doesn't occur more frequently than it does. But people will not mind being diverted from Glasgow to the Gobi Desert if only you tell them what's happening. Tell them merely that the delay is due to "operational reasons" and they'll all suspect that the Captain is drunk.

My views on this point were shared by the Station-master at Spagthorpe Junction. In one memorable B.B.C. programme he announced that the train then standing at Platform 1 was the train and the train arriving at Platform 2 was the Flying Scotsman which had frankly taken them all slightly by surprise.

It was also the attitude of the man in the queue at the time of the recent hi-jacking scare. It was of course a nuisance having to turn up at the airport two hours before take-off in order to be ransacked by an embarrassed teenage policeman, but we all saw the point. Nobody likes to find himself in mid-Atlantic sitting next to a fellow traveller whose underwear is full of hand grenades.

The Customs gentlemen, of course, boil a different kettle of fish. Getting through the Customs has developed into a battle of wits, but with all this ecology going around the rules of the game are becoming complex. "Have you anything to declare, Sir? Any uncut diamonds, gold bullion, narcotics, obscene literature, beeswax, nasturtium seeds, bird feathers, or dried meat?" If you're only carrying the permitted quota of dried meat you're allowed out through the green door of the Customs Shed, but those who fear they may be overstocked with beeswax must go out through the red. This sensible procedure has speeded things up a lot, but woe betide you if you don't declare anything and then get caught in a spot check.

Aficionados will remember the case of the medical student from Villars-sur-Bex. The Customs gentlemen at Gatwick bade him undo his Burberry presumably so that they could admire his waistcoat. This garment was subsequently found to contain 627 wrist watches, the existence of which V.-sur.-B. had omitted to mention. The Customs gentlemen naturally disapproved of this oversight, and so did the Recorder of London who granted V.-sur.-B. four years in which to reconsider his attitude. In the course of cross-examination, Sir Godfrey Russell Vick, Q.C. (defending), asked one of the Customs officers how his suspicions had been aroused. Had there been a tip-off from the Swiss authorities? Had some fence squealed? Or was it just the professional expertise and natural acumen of the Gatwick Customs? The officer scratched for a moment with the toe of perplexity upon the heel of embarrassment. "Sir Godfrey," he replied shyly, "it was none of these things. It had been a bumpy passage. They were self-winding watches, and the lad just stood there ticking like a plague of locusts."

By and large British Customs officials carry out a difficult task with courtesy and skill. So, indeed, do the Immigration authorities, though they have a more difficult task because politics enter into their game, and the stakes may be a good deal higher than with the Customs, particularly if you are trying to convince the officials that you are only one of a party of 137 East African Pakistani tourists seeking a week or two's respite in sun-drenched Solihull.

In America the rules are even tougher. In spite of all that friendly welcome to "the huddled masses yearning to breathe free" which is inscribed round the Statue of Liberty, Uncle Sam has grown a bit touchy about so many of the Mafia coming to visit their relations, and the immigration form you have to fill up is pretty stringent. Just after the war it used to be even more searching. Gilbert Harding took exception to Question 7 —"Do you intend to take up arms or offer violence against the Constitution of the U.S.A.?" "Sole purpose of visit" he declared firmly. But the Question I myself liked best was the last one of all that said, "In case you are illiterate you may ask for assistance in filling up this form."

As a matter of fact I never think the Americans need worry all that much about illegal immigrants. The normal process of arriving at J. F. Kennedy Airport ought to do as much to discourage them as any rules or red tape. What with stacking for two hours over the airport because the controllers are going slow, and trailing for three hours through the permanently temporary immigration hall because the clerks are going even slower, and then a journey on the airline courtesy coach which you hoped was going to take you from Panam via Branniff to United, but owing to your inability to understand the Bronx patois fetches you up outside the Ladies Lingerie Department of Saks Fifth Avenue, I think it's a miracle that anybody ever gets into the U.S.A. at all.

Mark you, we ourselves aren't always all that brilliant when the interests of travellers and workers are in conflict. The tourists off Cunard's *Carinthia* were once held up for three hours at the Liverpool Landing Stage because mice had been found in the dockers' canteen and the staff were out on strike, presumably for danger money. No wonder the Mersey Docks and Harbour Board are in trouble.

The French, of course, tackle the problem of red tape with a Gallic logic. One of the hazards of the travel trade, in which I used to earn my living, is the extent of the old boy net. This can occasionally enmesh you. "Why, goodness me," exclaims the Timbuctoo Airlines man at Bermuda Airport, "didn't we meet at last year's ASTA Conference in Tokyo?" "Yes, indeed." "Then come and have a drink. Abdul here will look after your tickets and passport." It isn't until you are half-way to Rio that you realise your passport is still in Abdul-here's pocket

The last time I performed this trick was at Le Bourget. When I realised what had happened I asked for the wayward passports to be registered on to me at the Poste Restante at Antibes. I duly went to collect them, only to be told by the Postmaster that by virtue of Sec. 52 of the 1927 Postal Code for the District of Alpes Maritimes a registered packet could not be handed over to a foreigner without production of his passport. Well, we could see which way this conversation was going, so my wife said, "Why not open the package yourself? You'll find the passports inside." "I am forbidden," replied the Postmaster gravely, "to open a registered package without the permission of the consignee." "But I *am* the consignee," I patiently explained. "Possibly," said the Postmaster sticking to his guns, "but you can't prove it without producing your passport." "Well, then," said my wife, "couldn't it be accidentally opened?" At that moment Mme. la Poste emerged from the back of the office. "Yes, indeed," she replied with an admiring glance at my wife. "Under Sec. 27 of the Code any registered package that becomes accidentally opened in transit must be resealed in the presence of the consignee. This accident will now occur." She thumped the package smartly on the counter; it burst open, and out came the passports. Back into the envelope they went, and the package was duly handed over to my wife, for whom I bought a well-earned bottle of Krug '28 at La Bonne Auberge outside.

Motto. Take your wife with you if you have to travel a lot, and are not good with regulations. And, incidentally, if she happens to be travelling anywhere without you and you want her back in a hurry, send her a copy of your local newspaper with a little paragraph cut out. Suspicious curiosity will put her on the next 'plane home.

# 14

# Travelling light

CHRISTMAS WILL soon be upon us, and once again we shall be regaled with pictures of Father Christmas zooming over the roof-tops in his reindeer sleigh, a vast sack of goodies slung over his shoulder.

Silly old man! Not only is the reindeer a notoriously unpredictable beast, particularly in the mating season, but the way in which that sack is over-loaded clearly contravenes all the IATA safety regulations for the carriage of goods by air.

Not, I suppose, that F. Christmas is any more worried about travel regulations than was King Charles II. His Majesty once invited himself to stay with Lord Eglington, who although naturally flattered by this mark of Royal favour was worried that his house might not be grand enough to accommodate his Sovereign. "Your Majesty will carry much baggage?" he inquired. "No," said the King, "just my night bag." "Not your usual Squadron of Horse and waggon-train?" asked Lord Eglington. "I call that my night bag," replied the King.

How lightly you travel depends, of course, on your reasons for travelling. My great-great-Uncle George was of a Carolian turn of mind, and his baggage, when he set off for Italy in 1830, included a heavy mahogany Davenport, the whole of the Works of Virgil, and a crate of Guinness. There was good reason for this. He had his eye on one of the Este girls of Modena, and he wanted to impress her parents that he was a man of substance, or, as it was called in those days, bottom.

The Owl and the Pussy Cat also had matrimony in mind when they went to sea in their beautiful pea-green boat but to take no more luggage than honey, money and a small guitar, seems to me to be going too far in the opposite direction.

Times, of course, have changed, and nowadays a lot of people travel by air. I've nothing against air-travel. It can be very exhilarating—breakfast in London, lunch in New York, and luggage in San Francisco. To obviate the dangers and delays inherent in being parted from your luggage, the Air Lines have approved a special carry-on suit-case for those who wish to travel really light. It needs two hefty air-hostesses to shove it under the seat, and you have to sit with your knees under your chin all the way to Bangkok. But you can flash through the airport at the speed of light, or could do until the hi-jacking scare encouraged the authorities to search everybody from top to toe.

Some notes of warning in this respect should now be sounded, particularly to married couples. Since not all husbands are constructed to the configuration of Mr. Mick McManus, wives should be discouraged from including sizeable bits of Stonehenge in their luggage. It should also be realized that two suit-cases weighing five tons each are more manageable than one of ten, particularly if you can trick your wife into carrying one of them.

But even the best trained wife needs watching. You have ejected the pieces of Stonehenge. You have finally persuaded her that she will not need nine pairs of shoes for a two-day Conference in Geneva. You have passed over the airport scales at the requisite weight, and have checked in unhindered. Your back is turned for an instant, and dammit there she is at your elbow with a vast coffee-table book on Seventeenth-Century Furniture, several bottles of duty-free liquor (which, as we all know, costs practically the same as dutiful liquor) and an armful of plastic Swiss Vatican Guards for the children.

A word now about children. Children do not travel light, and should, if possible, be dispatched by sea where they can be looked after properly, and, if needs be, locked up. Even if they stay at home they can give rise to difficulties because grandparents, not wishing to be lumbered with grandchildren in the event of their parents' death, demand that the parents do not travel in the same aircraft. So be it. But have a good look in your own suit-case before you set off on your separate ways, and make certain that nobody else's property has been inserted on the sly. Nothing is more down-toning than to assure a Customs Officer that you are travelling alone only to have him find your valise cluttered up with your wife's lacy black silk underwear.

There are some, of course, who travel light with an ulterior motive. More mature readers may remember a charming cabaret artiste named Miss Mañana. She used to appear in our music halls and night-clubs, before the war, clad only in a twelve-foot boa constrictor called Ziggy, whose function it was to take up strategic positions around her person. Upon reaching our shores in *The Queen Mary* for her first visit, Miss Mañana declared that her only luggage was the green canvas bag that contained Ziggy. She must, of course, have had other luggage elsewhere because you just can't walk down the Brompton Road in mid-November wearing nothing but a twelve-foot boa constrictor. But that was her story, and she stuck to it.

Well, the Southampton Customs people, with some lack of prescience, demanded that she open the bag. This she did, and out popped Ziggy. Everyone stood back respectfully, and Ziggy loped off in the direction of the Empress Dock. He was next seen at 6.30 the following evening by Mr. Howlett, one of the Bonded-goods Supervisors. He was taking his usual Johnny Walker and soda in the staff canteen when he suddenly observed Ziggy peering round the bottom of a cask of Worthington. Sensible man that he was, he didn't shout or make a fuss. He got up quietly, leaving his drink unfinished, and caught his bus back home to Netley. Shortly afterwards,

I believe, he signed the pledge and became a total abstainer.

Others travel light for fun. Students do it for the sake of economy, and the ones I see sleeping in Green Park on my way to work of a morning can travel even lighter than they used to because so few of them now seem to need room for razors, soap and hair-brushes.

A travel light situation confronted some friends of mine and myself when we visited the beaches of Normandy on 6 June 1944. As it was clear we might have to paddle ashore, and probably have unfriendly people throw things at us into the bargain, we did not wish to be embarrassed with more luggage than we could conveniently carry on our backs, or in the solitary Jeep that had been allotted to our H.Q. This was crammed full of petrol, ammunition, and other useful stand-bys. "Why petrol?" asked our Bombardier Bean. "If we can't borrow petrol off our neighbours, or prise it out of our opponents, we shall obviously have lost the battle, and there'll be no point in worrying. Let's take the petrol out and put in bread. Nobody else'll have that."

Nor had they, and our bread became currency. Indeed, Bombardier Bean, feeling the need for female company, went one evening into Bayeux with a loaf of Hovis under his arm. Not only did he get what he wanted, but he was given six eggs and a Camembert cheese as change. So, if you have to travel really light there are better things to do with bread than casting it on the waters.

# 15

# Travelling steerage

WHETHER YOU can afford it or not, you should always travel first class, unless they provide a de luxe or even higher class to which you will naturally transfer.

I was confirmed recently in this view by my old friend Charlie Cringleford. Now the Noble Lord, Lord Cringleford, though an excellent judge of port, is unfortunately an indifferent judge of racehorses and these two qualifications have prevented him from amassing much of a fortune. Although I was naturally delighted to find that he was a fellow passenger on a recent flight to New York, I was slightly surprised to see him heading like myself for the snobbier end of the plane. I, of course, was travelling at the shareholders' expense but Charlie, I knew, would be paying his own whack. I'm afraid, however, that I failed to disguise my surprise.

"Yes, indeed," he said when we were settled down to our Bloody Marys, "I used to travel steerage but I shall never do it again. I've learned my lesson. Last time I did it I had to spend seven hours in the heart of a Pakistani family reunion. Nomadic types too, they were. Fidgety. Up and down the whole time. And as for the food. Oh Lord! Nourishing enough but I've never really cared for gutta-percha sandwiches and purée of boot polish."

"And though of course I realise that they've got to pack 'em in, those kitchen chairs they give you in steerage class–" "Charlie," I said, "it's economy class, not steerage, and the seats are carefully designed to comply with international requirements. Nor is it really the fault of IATA that you yourself are constructed so nearly on the architectural principles of the Albert Hall that they have to take the plane apart and reconstruct it every time you want to wash your hands."

"All right," said Charlie, "I will ignore that insult although it reveals yet another reason for travelling first. I don't wish to appear unfriendly but I definitely do not relish standing for twenty minutes in the loo queue, squadged into the midst of a bevy of Pakistani beauties." Charlie paused. "I say, be a good fellow and ask the stewardess to put a smidgeon more celery salt in my next Bloody Mary and tell her, will you, that I'm going to have the Chambolle Musigny with my *sole Dieppoise* and the Aloxe Corton with the pheasant. Now, what about you?"

Charlie of course is right. Long distance air travel is remarkable value for money but the journey is never a joy-ride and if you have any regard for your comfort and, that most unattainable of all luxuries, privacy, the difference in price between first and economy class, though wide, is worth it.

The Russians, incidentally, have a different approach to the problem of the loo queue. I was flying once between Leningrad and Kiev and although the weather was perfect the pilot frequently switched on what I had by then learned to recognise as the "fasten your seat belt" sign. I eventually discovered the reason for this. To save weight and space, Russian designers have kept their aircraft pretty low on loos so the loo load factor is consequently high. When therefore the crew themselves want to wash their hands they slip on the seat-belt sign to ensure the competition is safely battened down.

The service and food in Russian aircraft is indescribable but this is because all Russian service and food is indescribable and not because the Russians have to comply with IATA regulations.

The service and food, however, in the Monarch class of BOAC is of a very high order indeed and a luncheon there can turn a routine journey into genuine pleasure. PanAm, Air India and KLM all run BOAC pretty close, but there's nothing new in standards such as these. The Paris service of Imperial Airways in the twenties was luxurious even by modern standards. The scoff was laid on to match and there wasn't, thank heavens, any Musak.

Today the VC 10 is the most comfortable aircraft flying, but even that machine would be hard put to beat the old Short Sunderland flying boat. This aeroplane had a separate dining-room, a comfortable dormitory upstairs and it brought you gently down on some romantic waterway each night of the eight-day journey to Australia. They also produced a marvellous curry tiffin but you were lucky not to get it in your lap if you got caught in a monsoon over the Arakan. The old bucket could bounce like blazes—even up in first class.

At sea, the class distinction used to be formidable. "Port out, Starboard home" gave memsahib the shady side of the ship and the word Posh to the English language. Cunard's pursers were instructed to have the steerage emigrants scrubbed on the quay-side at Liverpool in order to ensure that they arrived bugless in Boston. But the fare was only £4.10.

The first-class passengers, however, had to wear white ties for dinner but they had 26 brands of champagne to choose from. Their linen sheets were changed each night though not, we hope, scrubbed.

Most new passenger liners today are classless. A few, like *QE2*, are dual purpose ships; two classes across the Atlantic and classless whilst cruising. This interchangeability makes it difficult to persuade people to travel first because the class distinction appears to be so slight. But I can assure you it's worth it because in the real first class you get limitless caviare and a nice little fridge in your stateroom.

The *QE2*'s problem arises again in our trains. British Railways' new rolling stock is nearly as comfortable in second class as it is in first but although both classes invariably go on strike at the same time, there's still a valid reason for travelling first and that, of course, is breakfast.

BR's breakfast is a wonderful meal and if they could only serve breakfast at lunch and dinner, British Rail would have the best mobile cuisine in the world. Not that their other meals are all that bad. They do occasionally serve up the piece of cod that passeth all understanding but a lot may be forgiven a chef who has to juggle with boiling fat at 80 m.p.h.

Always travel first class rail between Washington and New York; it's much more comfortable than the air and oddly enough it's faster. Be a devil, too, and travel de luxe by CPR from Vancouver. Their scenic car gives you a view of the Rockies that's even more spectacular than the brochure proclaims and it's nice having a moose watching you shave.

It's difficult to define class in hotels. Too many hotels are now just body-servicing units and luxury consists in being able to leave a hotel without standing in line for twenty minutes for the privilege of paying your bill. I'm all for electric razor sockets, of course, as well as ice-making machines in the passage, but sometimes I miss the old-fashioned night-porter and his comments on the 3.30 at Kempton Park.

In most modern hotels real luxury can only mean real service. I own a rather disreputable pair of leather slippers which are useful for kicking-off in aeroplanes. Despite my wife's protests that we should lose face, I put them outside our door to be cleaned when we were last staying in the superb Mandarin Hotel in Hong Kong. They were duly returned in the morning, not only shining like the Morning Star but soled and heeled as well. That I call très grande luxe.

But luxury in travel is relative. Was the outside of the Edinburgh stage coach in a howling blizzard over the Yorkshire moors considered grander than the sardine-packed and pongful interior? And in any case, both classes ran an equal risk of being held up by Dick Turpin proclaiming, "Your money or your life" which is the olde Englishe for "Excuse please, if you do not fly this aircraft to Cuba immediately, I will be forced to blow out your brains."

I must apologise to all potential steerage passengers for the bloatedly plutocratic advice that I have been offering. I should, however, also like to offer one final word by way of recompense.

BOAC own a miraculous piece of tele-communication juju named Boadicea which, at the punch of a key, can tell you the load factor of next Wednesday's flight out of Boston or the names of those who are travelling first-class this afternoon to Johannesburg. One day I was watching Boadicea at work and up on the screen popped the name of my old friend Jimmy X, apparently South Africa-bound. I remarked to BOAC's men, "I did not realise that my friend X had interests in the Cape." "No," said BOAC, "You have misread the data. Observe the asterisk against your friend's name. That indicates he is disembarking in Rome."

Two days later I ran across Lady X at a party. "And how is that old rascal Jimmy enjoying himself in Rome?" enquired Mr. Know All. "Rome?" replied a slightly puzzled Lady X. "Jimmy's not in Rome. He's fishing up in Scotland."

You do not run that sort of risk in steerage.

# 16

# Down with August !

YOU MAY have noticed that they've changed the date of the August Bank Holiday. It used to be the eighth Monday after Trinity, but now it tends to fall on the first Monday before Muckspreading, or thereabouts. This has naturally proved confusing, so most people take both Mondays off just to make sure.

Come to think of it, most people seem to take the whole of August off, anyway. You can't get anything done, although, oddly enough, there are still plenty of people around who are ready to do you. Bills continue to glide through the letter-box, but if you ring up and say that you can't possibly have had 127 trunk calls to Wolverhampton in one week because your phone was out of order, they say they're sorry but the computer's gone on holiday, and will you please complain again in September.

Parking tickets continue to fall as thick as leaves in Vallombrosa, but if you go round to explain that it can't be you they're grumbling about because your car has been in the garage for three months waiting for a spare part, you'll find the office shut, for the hols, and a notice saying, "Try Wandsworth Civic Centre".

Frankly, I don't understand this. When you consider all the awful things that have happened to us in August you'd have thought that we would be on our toes, and ready to take on all comers. Not a bit of it. And the rot didn't set in yesterday, either.

Go back to 55 BC, and what do we find? We find Julius Caesar turning up uninvited on the beach at Broadstairs right in the middle of the August holidays. This was not only tiresome, but tactless. Although his nephew, Augustus, named the month of August after himself, he had magnanimously named July after Julius. July, therefore, would have been a more fitting month for the outing. But no, August it was, and bless me if Caesar wasn't back again the next August, and with a much stronger cast; five Legions and 2,000 Cavalry, no less. All tourist towns like repeat business, but that must have been a bit much for the back streets of Broadstairs, and everyone was obviously relieved when Caesar pushed off to the north. Unfortunately he got bogged down at Dagenham, which, as any Ford shareholder could have told him, was only to be expected. At Colchester worse befell. There Caesar lost his 2 i/c., C. Publius Severus, poisoned by a bad oyster. August you see; no "R" in the month.

And so it went on. In August 1667 the Dutch Fleet sailed up the Medway, and scant good came of that. Nobody paying attention, that was the trouble. Just as nobody was paying attention when the Great Train Robbery was pulled off in August 1963, or when Lord Beaverbrook bought *The Daily Express* in the August of 1916.

Sir Francis Drake was the man largely responsible for this couldn't-care-less approach. It was of course in August that he put paid to the Spanish Armada, having refused to accelerate his game of bowls for a lot of bumptious dagoes. Actually, this was just a simple piece of West Country one-upmanship on Drake's part, and the silly foreigners fell for it. So far from being caught on the hop, Sir Francis had everything nicely laid on; all kegs properly powdered, all drums at the ready, and the Cap'n very far from sleeping there below. Even in 1588 we were not quite so casual as we seemed.

I don't think, however, that this dawned on the Spaniards, or on any of their successors who have subsequently wished us ill. August, they felt, would automatically catch us napping, and was therefore the right time of the year to try and do us a mischief. And, boy, have they tried!

The Kaiser tried in August 1914. Our grandparents were paddling at Broadstairs, but Winston assures us in his little book that "the Army was ready, the Navy was ready, the Civil Service was ready; all my plans worked perfectly". Even allowing for Churchillian hyperbole, they didn't work so badly at that.

Nor did they in 1939. There were, of course, a few lacunae. Hitler became Chancellor of the German Reich in 1934 (guess when? 2 August) and subsequently entered into his non-aggression Pact with Russia in 1939 (guess when? 23 August). In consequence my regiment was mobilised on 24 August—or almost. What actually happened was that the sub-postmistress who was due to send off our mobilisation papers must have been on holiday herself, and my own marching orders turned up so late that they nearly had to start the War without me. But my C.O. was very nice about it, and said it really didn't matter at all.

We certainly do lay ourselves open for trouble in August. We invite disaster, and are peeved when we get it. We beaver away in secret behind the scenes, and are then hurt if nobody takes us seriously. During World War I Bert Thomas produced a cartoon of a whimsical and battered Tommy lighting his pipe, and under it the caption "'Arf a mo', Kaiser". This sentiment, infuriating to our enemies and to such friends as we still possess, is a source of smug satisfaction to ourselves. It typifies, we like to think, our feeling for expert improvisation, and our refusal, like Sir Francis Drake, to be jockeyed into rearranging our priorities. But I still think it's tempting Providence.

In the Summer of 1944 I was staying with a few friends near a village called Douvres la Deliverande, in Normandy. Unfortunately it still harboured some Germans whose presence had been over-looked by the 3rd Canadian Division on their way up North. The Germans, in their rather caddish manner, started to take pot-shots at our Brigadier on his way to the Mobile Bath Unit. "Get rid of them", he said, "at once". We planned an operation for the next evening, Thursday, at 9 p.m. We consulted our advisers. Bombardier Bean shook his head, sadly. "Thursday, at 2100 hours?", he said. "No, Sir, sorry, Sir. Not on, Sir. That's ITMA".

ITMA was a radio programme of inspired lunacy. It soon became so popular that nobody could be expected to go into battle whilst it was on the air. The enemy discovered this, and attacked so frequently at 9 p.m. on a Thursday that ITMA had to be broadcast at differing times and dates. This was carrying the doctrines of Sir Francis Drake and Bert Thomas to extremes.

Even after the War we persisted in thinking that just because we were all on holiday in August ourselves, people would leave us alone. The Berlin crisis, the confrontation with Nasser, and the Persian oil row of 1951, all ought to have reminded us how vulnerable we still are in August. Admittedly this August hasn't been so bad as some, but I'm glad it's over and done with, all the same. On the Glorious Twelfth it was reported from the Moors that the grouse seemed a little bit jumpy. A day or two later the same trouble was reported about the Dollar. The weather was, as usual, summery. Our local Bring and Buy Sale was not just washed out—it was sluiced out. But *sluiced*. But then, the weather always is vile in August; September is infinitely better. Charles II maintained that a man could be usefully employed out of doors in England for more days than in any other country in the world, and although I am not sure I would consider Charles II an expert on employment *out* of doors, I think he had a point. But even he thought nothing of August. He said it gave him gout.

Nasser, Hitler, the Kaiser, and now gout. It's just too much. I think that August should be abolished.

# 17

# More blessed to give than to receive

OUR BRANCH of the Women's Institute was holding a jumble sale. "Get rid of anything not worth keeping, yet too good to give away", the posters proclaimed. "Don't forget to bring your husband".

I didn't care much for this implication, but had agreed, nevertheless, to accompany my wife to the sale because we both wanted to see what fate might befall an exquisitely carved walnut whatnot which we were putting up for disposal on Mrs. Wicksteed's stall. It had been a Christmas present some years back, and we had never discovered what it was actually meant for. My children said that it was obviously a whatnot, and a collector's piece at that, but we had decided, nonetheless, that it would have to be surrendered.

When we had eventually located Mrs. Wicksteed's stall we found that our whatnot was the only merchandise still unsold. "There now," I said, "I was afraid, Mrs. Wicksteed, that not even an entrepreneuse like you would be able to off-load such a dreadful bit of junk as that. Isn't it amazing the rubbish that people give you?" Mrs. W. said nothing, but pursed her lips, and it wasn't until we were half way home that I remembered that it was she who had given us the whatnot.

Many people must have fallen into a similar trap. Not only

is it more blessed to give than to receive, but it is also a great deal easier. The methods of avoiding the trap are many and varied. All demand finesse—some call for bravado.

Take, for instance, the American poetess Phyllis McGinley. She, at least, runs no risk of being misunderstood.

> *Leave for me* [she sings],
> *Some minor bauble underneath the tree,*
> *Perhaps a gilt-edged bond,*
> *Some modest pearl,*
> *Or simple diamond.*

My friend, Charlie Cringleford, thinks along the same lines, but he is not quite so subtle as Miss McGinley. "Listen," he bellowed down the telephone into my pre-Christmas ear, "what, pray, is Santa Mancroft thinking of putting into my stocking this year?"

"I'm giving you a case of whisky, which you do not deserve," I said. "What are you giving me?"

"I have allotted you," said Charlie, "a dozen bottles of the 1964 Marcobrunnen Beerenauslese. A bit above your station, I'm afraid, but we'll let that pass."

"Charlie," I exclaimed, "you know perfectly well that I can't drink hock; it makes my colly wobble."

"Precisely," said Charlie, "and I don't propose that you should. I, whose palate is far more cultivated than yours, will enjoy this superb Rheingau whilst you are slupping down the undistinguished whisky you propose to give me. Both of us will get the present we deserve, and good money will be saved in the costs of transportation."

I realised that this ploy, though vulgar, had merit. I cast my mind back to the previous Christmas and remembered the tie that Aunt Hetty had given me. I wore it one night to the House of Lords during the Report Stage of the Immigration Bill, and several of their Lordships complained to the Whips. I remembered the five copies of Antonia Fraser's *Mary, Queen of Scots* which I had received the year before. Greatly though I admire both ladies (but for different reasons) one copy would have sufficed. There was also Miss Protheroe's tea-cosy, and the Cyprus sherry from the garage. I also remembered Mrs. Wicksteed's whatnot. I would have felt more blessed without any of them.

This Christmas, then, I decided to follow Charlie's example. I issued a family encyclical. No presents for Pater. (I have to pay for them myself, anyway.) "But won't you look a little forsaken round the tree whilst we are opening ours?" (They had already ordered their presents from me after a token consultation.) "I shall survive," I replied with dignity.

Straight-grained pipes, Cashmere waistcoats, finely embroidered slippers, after-shave pong by the hogshead and much other enviable merchandise flowed my way last Christmas. The device was, of course, disguised. The pipes were gift-wrapped and carried a label reading, "With all good wishes from the Archbishop of Canterbury". The slippers said: "Many thanks for all your loyal support. Bravo! Ted". The waistcoat bore witness to the fact that the Lord Mayor and Lady Mayoress not only wished me a Happy Christmas, but a Prosperous New Year as well. I don't know if anyone was actually convinced by this tactic, but I do know that I felt more blessed to receive for once something that I really wanted.

I had, however, reckoned without Aunt Hetty. She slipped through the net, but this time, bless her old heart, she gave me a present that was genuinely welcome, namely a gramophone record voucher. I went round to our local supermarket to swap it for a new recording of the Mozart horn concertos.

Two notices there caught my eye. One proclaimed that goods purchased by a husband alone on a Saturday could be exchanged by a wife between 10 and 2 on a Monday. This struck me as a new and useful variation on the theme. The other notice stated that luncheon vouchers were accepted. Luncheon vouchers now rate as currency. You can exchange them not only for lunch, but for theatre tickets, nylons, gramophone records and bottles of whisky.

On second thoughts, then, I decided to exchange Aunt Hetty's record voucher for luncheon vouchers to exchange for whisky to allot to Charlie Cringleford next Christmas.

And if he's behaved himself over the year I will also give him my trading stamps, which he can exchange for whisky tumblers at his local garage and then give back to me.

# 18

# The Common Market Sausage

THOUGH I say it myself as shouldn't, I am one of the few people who really understand all the implications of our entry into the Common Market.

Last night I was explaining some of these to Percy, my neighbour's pigman, for whom there are still a few grey areas. "You see, Percy," I said, "for all official Common Market budgeting, as well as for agricultural price guarantees, the Six use the 'unit of account' which is equal to the artificial gold exchange rate of the undiscounted pre-August dollar. The Commission is also hoping to re-value the unit upwards by some three and a half per cent." Percy thanked me courteously, and bicycled off in the direction of the Seven Bells.

Next morning he hailed me from the litter-bin where he was helping a Landrace sow through some little local difficulties. "Tell me," he said, "now that we're in this little old Market, will they be selling sausages to us, or us to them?"

When you think of the time, money and effort which the Government has spent on trying to explain what the EEC is all about, it's sad to find that even a clear-headed chap like Percy is still confused about sausages. Perhaps he's been listening to Mr. Harold Wilson in mid mind-change.

Before we move into the sausage market, however, there are

one or two more important things which we have to sell to Europe, and the first of these is the English language. English will have to become the common language of the Market, however much the others may try to resist it. I agree that French is a very pretty language, especially useful, as Mark Twain pointed out, for giving recitations, and getting money out of middle-aged ladies. But it's not so precise a language as English. This, of course, is why French is the language of diplomacy. You can soar and dip like a seagull with your *tours d'horizon*, your *démarches*, *détentes*, and *aides-mémoire*, and the *chers colleagues* needn't get pinned down with anything too precise. That may be all right for the Quai d'Orsay, but not for sausages. Mongénéral realised this well enough, and the risk of French being trumped as a European language was, I believe, one of the chief reasons for his intransigence about Britain's entry into the Common Market.

German is a more precise language than French, but a few people with long memories still don't like to hear or speak it. And Italian, though charming, is only spoken by Italians and American policemen. And no one in his right mind would try to learn Dutch. The Dutch know this, and, in consequence, all speak fluent English.

So English it has to be. But English English—not American English. The Americans have a neat turn of phrase, and have enriched our language. But put them round a conference table, or give them a market survey to draft, and they become circumlocuitously incomprehensible. Mrs. Thrale reproved Dr. Johnson for using words like "alexipharmic" and "fugacious", but even he would have frowned upon the Americans for calling a useful meeting a "meaningful encounter", or referring to a private chat as an "interfacial involvement".

At a sales conference which I attended recently in Brussels it was discovered that there is no precise distinction in the Scandinavian languages between sales promotion, advertising and public relations. The Dutch, the French and the Italians all had a go at explaining these differences to our confused Vikings, but when we moved into English the task became noticeably easier. You tell a girl how pretty she is, and how much you would like her to dine with you; that (we explained) is sales promotion. If, on the other hand, you tell her what a fine chap you are, and how much she would enjoy dining with you, that's advertising. But if she tells you how much she's heard your praises sung, and will you please take her out to dinner, then that, of course, is public relations.

So be it. Our first task is to sell English to the Europeans as the language of the Common Market. Fortunately it already happens to be the second language of most of the world, and in any case there's no need to apologise for the language of Shakespeare, Winston, and the Authorised Version of the Bible.

The next thing we've got to sell to Europe is the English system of Government. Just now this may not be quite so easy to put over. Our European colleagues may have been a little unedified by the spectacle of Honourable Members entangled on the Floor of the House of Commons with the best of two falls, two submissions, or a knock-out to decide the winner. But other European Parliaments have also had their innocent diversions. Before the War, when Governments changed rapidly in France, one elderly statesman who had nodded off on a warm afternoon in the Chamber awoke to find he had been Prime Minister twice. And an Italian Deputy from the South once felt compelled to stand on his head on the back benches in order to catch the Speaker's eye.

But by and large British administration, and the counter-balances between legislature and executive, works as well as, if not better than, any other. It is also probably less corrupt because that splendid institution, the Parliamentary Question, keeps Whitehall on its toes. The gentleman in Whitehall may not (as Douglas Jay once remarked to his cost) actually know best, but he does know better than some foreigners how to make the machinery of Government work. So when it comes to manning the Euro-sausage Control Commission, and such like, let us try and persuade our friends that British practices should prevail, and that British civil servants and politicians should do much of the prevailing. And if we can sell them a little British protocol, and even a little pomp and circumstance as well, then so much the better.

When we start trying to sell them our ships, and shoes, and sealing wax, we shall find the going tougher. I recently attended a Seminar on "Selling in the Seventies". The car park outside the hall was packed with Fiats, Citroens, Volvos, Saabs and Volkswagens, and I pondered anxiously on the seventeen things that had gone wrong with my new British car within a fortnight of delivery.

I don't like to cry stinking fish, but we're moving into a highly sophisticated market where delivery dates and after-sales service really matter. We're nothing like as bad in this respect as some of our competitors in Europe, for obvious reasons, try to make out. But too many of our goods still fall apart too easily, and too many spare parts don't appear to exist.

Time was when the word "trade" was not music to the ears of the English gentleman. Lord Chesterfield would not sit at table with anyone engaged in Trade. In *The Last Chronicle of Barset* the butler is reproved for not sending the Chairman of the local brewery round to the tradesmen's entrance. Napoleon called us a nation of shopkeepers, but I'm never quite clear whether he intended it as a compliment, or an insult. Nevertheless, some members of the Upper Crust have kept a careful eye on the export market. The Crusaders, whilst busy around Jerusalem, introduced British woollen textiles to the Levant. The English Milord came back from the Grand Tour with the raw material for some of the finest private art collections in the world, and at knock-down prices, too. In return he introduced Scotch whisky to Europe, and look what that's done for the balance of payments. Commercially we're not such chumps as people like to make out, but we shall certainly have to keep our wits about us.

I met Percy outside the Seven Bells after last Sunday's British Legion parade. "Listen to this," he said, brandishing his newspaper. "A British perfume company which exported hundreds of gallons of toilet-water to Russia was paid with hundreds of pairs of gum-boots. And a chemical firm up in the North did an exchange deal with Egypt, and got a warehouse filled with camel saddles in return. The chemical firm's chap in Nigeria thought he might trade the camel saddles in Lagos, but the only snag was that he had a ship-load of cement left over from another deal. It's all here in the paper," said Percy, "so it must be true. And what I want to know is this. The wife and I are going to the Costa Brava for our holiday. Can I pay for my ticket with sausages?"

I'm afraid we've got a lot more work to do on Percy.

# 19

# Pray silence

"MR. CHAIRMAN," roars the Toastmaster, "Your Grace, Your Eminence, Your Beatitude, Your Worships, Aldermen, Sheriffs, My Lords, Ladies and Gentlemen, pray silence for Sir Bert Buggins, Holder of the Ruritanian Order of Chastity Fourth Class, Knight Grand Cross of the Order of St. Tom, St. Dick and St. Harry, and Prime Warden of the Worshipful Company of Rathole Bunger-Uppers, who will propose the Toast to the Guests."

Our Bert, who's been waiting twenty years for this occasion, clambers unsteadily to his feet, blows into the microphone to see if it's working, prays to heaven he'll be able to remember at least some of that gullet-busting preamble, and launches into his carefully prepared impromptu speech.

Behind him the Toastmaster pulls Bert's chair back, drapes an immaculate white glove over an immaculate red sleeve, and does his best to look amused at Bert's halting version of the story about the Christian, the lion, and the after-dinner speech which he is now hearing for the seven hundred and forty-third time.

The Toastmaster is a singularly British creation. Correction: English. Further correction: London. There are, I believe, a few good Toastmasters lurking in the Provinces, and if the provincials haven't got one handy, the R.S.M. from the local Territorial Regiment may be able to oblige. If things are really desperate, the Headwaiter at the Grand Hotel can probably weigh in with the resounding accents of Barcelona, or Milan, but if you want the job done properly you'd better get a man down from London.

Here you will be faced with a slight problem, for no less than five organisations are eagerly seeking your custom. There's the Society of London Toastmasters, founded in 1950, with twenty-five members; there's the Association of Toastmasters & Masters of Ceremonies; there's the Toastmasters & M.C.'s Federation; there's also the London Guild of Toastmasters; and, finally, there's the Guild of Professional Toastmasters. And, believe it or not, these five bodies, in toto, embrace scarcely more than a hundred members. One would have thought, therefore, that they would be well advised to get together and pool their talents.

Why do I speak so positively, and what authority have I to do so? I must declare an interest. I have just retired, after nearly twenty years, as Honorary Toastmaster to the Society of London Toastmasters. I've thoroughly enjoyed the job, I've been proud to hold the title, and I've made a lot of very good friends. But enough, I feel, is enough.

Not that the work has been all that onerous. The most I've had to do is to act as Toastmaster at the Society's annual Christmas dinner; and, whilst I have often made a nonsense of this particular task, I have, in turn, been able to note that not all Toastmasters can be classed as brilliant after-dinner speakers. I have also been able to discover why a Toastmaster is a useful man to have around.

The Americans also have Toastmasters, but these are of a different breed. They are chatter-uppers; glad-handers; verbal back-slappers; and their job it is to put an audience on good terms with itself. This is something the Americans dearly love to do, even though the doing of it invariably lengthens the proceedings by at least a couple of hours. When in evening dress, however, the Americans like to proceed slowly.

The British Toastmaster chats nobody up. Not for nothing is "*omnium cum dignitate*" the motto of our Society. Apart from the formalities of announcement, a Toastmaster should never open his mouth, though I do remember one occasion when a Toastmaster was so carried away by a speech about the plight of ex-service pensioners that he seized the microphone from the speaker and launched into a powerful postscript, drawn from his own experiences. The effect was tremendous, but he was never invited to repeat it.

The best way of discovering why a Toastmaster is necessary is to attend a function where the organisers think he's not. The result is invariably a shambles.

We British are a tidy people. We are fond of protocol though we dislike pomposity. We approve of formality but we do not like it to be unnecessarily protracted. Hence the Toastmaster.

The hosts at your dinner have taken much trouble to organise the function. The ladies have put on their prettiest dresses. The chef has done his best with his *Escalopines de Veau St. Jacques.* So why not complete the picture and have a Toastmaster to see that the guests are properly announced, the company correctly marshalled, and the speakers brought to their feet in due order? And if some little local difficulty should crop up—if a waiter should mistakenly spill too much soup over your wife's dress, or Bert Buggins a little too much Scotch into himself—then just pass the word to the Toastmaster and nobody will know that anything is amiss.

Sometimes, a crisis can be more serious. On two occasions, alas, I have known a speaker collapse in the middle of a speech; and on both occasions the Toastmaster, by tact and quickness of wit, managed to avert what might otherwise have been an unhappy scene.

How do you get hold of a Toastmaster? If you don't yourself know a Toastmaster personally, discuss the matter with the Banqueting Manager of any big hotel. He probably has a pet Toastmaster whom he'll recommend. But there's no hard-and-fast rule about this, and no closed shop. Ring up, then, any Toastmaster you like. His wife will invariably answer the 'phone. That's her job. If her husband doesn't happen to be free on your particular night, she'll give you the name of the next man down the list. They work to an agreed rota. There are now even one or two lady Toastmistresses, and I hope their husbands do the same for them in reverse, but goodness knows how the bachelors get on.

How did Toastmasters originate? Their history is hazy. The first Toastmaster was, I suppose, Stentor the Herald. Skipping a few centuries, we learn that at Edward II's first State Banquet, the official announcements were made by his favourite, Piers de Gaveston, about whom the less said the better. At George IV's Coronation Breakfast, the job was done by the Earl of Halidon, who was subsequently found behind a dirty linen-basket drunk (I'm afraid) as a lord. And, believe it or not, the poet Robbie Burns was once a Toastmaster. But, by and large, the Toastmaster as we now know him is a comparatively modern invention.

How do you become a Toastmaster? In former days, quite a few of them appear to have been unsuccessful baritones on Eastbourne Pier, but now they're a more professional lot. Some are the sons of Toastmasters. Some are coming up through the trainee ranks of the catering trade. This is as it should be, because there is a close connection between Toastmaster, Banqueting Manager, Headwaiter and Chef. A few Toastmasters are ex-headwaiters, civic macebearers, or beadles of City Livery Companies. In all cases, new candidates are—in our lot, at any rate—rigorously vetted.

How much do they earn? I've never had the effrontery to ask. A successful man might do a trade-show in the morning, followed by a business luncheon at midday; then a cocktail-party in the West End, and a City banquet in the evening. Even so, the fees are not princely, and the wear and tear on white ties and red coats, must be dreadful. Not all Toastmasters, of course, are as busy as that. Some have other jobs during the day, in Directors' lunch-rooms and the like. One of our members winds the clocks in the Head Office of a big foreign bank, and he says that it's driving him mad. But most of them work full-time and are rarely back home in Northwood before dawn.

There are naturally horses for courses. Some Toastmasters specialise in Masonic and Rotary work. Others are popular in the Jewish community. Some, I'm sorry to say, will put on funny hats and do "Knees up, Mother Brown". All can judge when a full and flowery treatment is in order, or when slightly less protocol would fill the bill.

And talking of bills, I remember that the Toastmaster who officiated at my stepdaughter's wedding forgot to send in his. I wrote in due course and asked him to let me know what I owed him. "Nothing," he replied. His services were his personal wedding-present to the bride and bridegroom.

They're a very nice body of men, these Toastmasters, and I envy my successor.

# 20

# Up the Alps

THE MIGRATORY season is upon us, and birds and business-men will soon be winging their way to the sun. British swifts and swallows will be heading for Algeria, and British stock-brokers for the Bahamas, where they will plod round the golf-course discussing with other stockbrokers the beauties of Partly Convertible Unsecured Loan Stock.

Cohorts of Canadian bankers will descend upon Barbados to refloat with other bankers the zloty and the yen, whilst enjoy-ing a Bloody Mary at Cobblers Cove, or swimming in a sea of tepid Bouillabaisse. American businessmen will head for Miami Beach, most of them to the Fontainbleu (pronounced bloo) Hotel. This establishment is about the size of Birmingham, though not quite so cosy. It is, however, one of the few hotels in Miami where you don't have to start queuing for Wednes-day's lunch at about 6 o'clock on Tuesday evening. Movie Moguls will head for Acapulco, property magnates for Tel Aviv, and brewers for the Carlton at Cannes.

My friend Charlie Cringleford is off to Switzerland, and this surprises me. Although the Alps are obviously ideal for Conservative M.P.s and other young in heart, they don't strike me as being particularly suitable for a tycoon of Charlie's calibre.

"Charlie," I said, "will you really be able to unwind at St. Moritz?"

"I'm not going to the Alps to unwind," he replied. "Indeed, throughout a fairly busy life I have managed to save a lot of time by *not* unwinding."

"Very well, but won't you find the Swiss a little dull?"

"Don't be silly," said Charlie, "you don't go to St. Moritz to meet the Swiss, any more than you go to Montego Bay to meet Jamaicans. You go to meet other businessmen, and the best way to strike up a conversation is by asking if you can borrow Tuesday's *Financial Times*, or whether anyone knows the time at which the Stock Exchange opens in Tokyo."

"Nevertheless," he continued, "I do not happen to share the jaundiced view of the Swiss that is advanced by people like Lord Arran. Admittedly the Swiss are not a dazzling race. In this respect they differ from the Italians who, in spite of a thousand years of cloak, dagger, and general skullduggery, have given us Leonardo, Michelangelo and Dante, Rigoletto, the Medici, and Milan Cathedral. After a thousand years of good order and neutrality, the most significant Swiss contribution to civilisation is, we are told, the cuckoo clock."

"*And* the numbered bank account," I added, trying to be helpful.

"Ah, yes," said Charlie, "how right you are—for where would places like Annabel's be without the numbered bank account? Not, of course, that I would ever dare to bandy words with a Swiss banker. He'd see me off in a trice!" This was strong talk, because the Noble Lord, Lord Cringleford, is not notably seeoffable.

I changed my tack. "You go for the ski-ing, then?" I asked.

"Don't be absurd!" he replied. "Nobody but a potential suicide would ever dream of touching a pair of skis—though, mark you, I think the difficulties of ski-ing are over-rated. There are really only three things to learn; how to put on your skis, how to slide downhill, and how to walk along the hospital corridor. But as you know, I myself don't approve of exercise of any kind. Indeed, the only exercise I ever take is walking up hospital stairs to visit friends who've damaged themselves by taking exercise."

"The climate, then?" I ventured.

"Also over-rated" he replied, "particularly the snow. Snowflakes are like people—individually charming, but a confounded nuisance in large numbers. I grant you, however, that some may consider the climate of Switzerland invigorating. A day on the nursery slopes can make a woman of forty look like a man of thirty".

"Then I'm beginning to wonder what you really *are* going for. The natural beauties of the place, perhaps?" I asked.

"You are not referring, I trust." Charlie replied, "to all those little frippets drinking hot chocolate at the *après-ski*, or holding hands in the Palace Hotel with Debrett, the Almanack de Gotha, and the ski-ing instructors? No, no, my boy. I'm too proud a man for that sort of thing; too decent, too loyal—and too old. Besides, not even the nobility stand a chance against those ski-ing instructors, with their nods, and becks, and wreathed smiles. The adultery rate in Alpine ski resorts must be very high indeed—higher even than in Gloucestershire. I believe that the barman at the Suvretta shakes a cocktail called an Aphrodisia. It's alleged to make you see double and feel single. Most ski-instructors pretend to be single, but they are in fact quite married, and their wives must be amongst the most adulterated women in Europe. No, no, not that sort of natural beauty."

"The mountains, then?"

Charlie suddenly beamed. "Yes, indeed—the mountains. You've got it at last. I love the mountains. Their beauty never fails to fascinate. They're so pure, and hard, and silent. *So* unlike my colleagues on the Board of Amalgamated!"

Charlie has been Chairman of Amalgamated for nearly ten years, but it's been an uneasy reign, because Charlie is not an easy ruler. His co-directors, for instance, have not forgotten the time he tried to appoint his poodle to a non-executive directorship on their Board. Charlie argued in vain that the dog's eager response to a pat on the back, its love of watching others work, and its ability to look wise whilst remaining silent, made it a natural candidate for the post.

I bore these facts in mind. "I see what you mean about the mountains, Charlie," I said, "but for a busy man like you, accepting as you do the theory that the absent are always in the wrong, surely the Alps are a little inaccessible? Three hours on the funicular? The plane over-booked?"

"And thank Heaven for that," said Charlie, with a thump on the bar that made the glasses bounce. "That's just why I go there. Do you know, the Board actually killed off my predecessor by keeping him constantly in the air. They would send him off to represent the Company at some Seminar in San Francisco, and as soon as he was off the plane they'd have him up in the air again for a Conference in Bangkok, only to call him back as soon as he arrived. He had a coronary in next to no time, which was just what the Board intended. (He wouldn't retire, and was blocking promotion.) Very clever of them. British management isn't always as stupid as *The Economist* likes to make out. Not as clever as the Swiss, of course. *They*'re real professionals in everything they touch, and that's why I'm so fond of Switzerland. Off with you, then, to the Caribbean, if you're so minded, but you'll note that the best hotels there are always the ones where the staff has been trained by the Swiss. Real professionals, as I say. How I dislike amateurs! Whether it be drinking hot chocolate, or teaching ski-ing, committing adultery, or making money out of tourists, give me the professional every time."

"By the way," he said, after a pause for refreshment, "where are you yourself off to this winter? You'd better make some show of unwinding, even if, as we all know, you've never been in any real danger of getting wound up in the first place. Why not come out with me to the Alps?"

"Thank you for the kind thought," I said, "but as a matter of fact I propose to stay at home and cultivate my garden."

There was a long pause. "You may well be right," my friend eventually observed. "As far as I can remember, your garden is always a proper mess at the turn of the year. But there's something else you ought to bear in mind. Is there not a risk that your proposed course of action may give unwarranted comfort to your neighbours? May they not think they have at last seen the real you—contemplative, calm, well-organised—and broke?"

# 21

# The Graduate in Business

I WAS engaged to address the Students' Union of Kyoto University on the subject of Containerisation and Bulk Cargoes in the Pacific Trade. Unfortunately my speech could not be delivered and this seemed to me a pity because I thought it contained some really pulse-quickening stuff.

On the night of my arrival, however, the students of Kyoto University were busily engaged in burning their University to the ground. Mr. Okomoto, the Dean of Extramural Studies, explained to me during intervals of running out with glasses of beer for the firemen, that half the students were protesting against the continued occupation of Okinawa by the Americans, and the other half against the quality of the vegetables in the Freshmen's canteen. Whilst he was out of his room I happened to glance at a chart on his wall, and I noticed with interest that nearly twice as many Japanese graduates seem to choose business as a career as do their counterparts in Britain or America.

I wanted to know more about this because the University graduates' lack of interest in business is something that has been worrying us all here in Britain for quite a while. The University Grants Committee issues reports; the Business Graduates' Association, the British Institute of Management and old uncle Unilever and all publish pamphlets. The CBI and the Institute of Directors furrow their corporate brows; gurus from the Manchester Business School fly over to see what their opposite numbers at the Harvard Business School and MIT are up to; youngish Mr. Wedgwood Benn relights his pipe and gazes intently at the cameras. But the Situation Gets No Better. It seems that whilst all sensible graduates are only too happy to shop at Marks & Spencers, not quite so many of them are prepared to work there, particularly if the job involves selling socks on a Saturday morning when their friends are all out of the golf course.

The Institute of Marketing, of which I was once President, organised a Symposium, and we spent the whole day worrying away like billy-o. The key-note speech was made by the sales manager of a mail order business in the Midlands. He thought that however much lip-service we might pay to the idea, there was really no place for the university graduate in business. Well, all right, he was aware that business embraces everything from selling stocks to selling socks so that in that case one or two graduates might be allowed to rub along in the Banks or on the Stock Exchange, or in Lloyd's, and if your Uncle Charlie happens to be managing director of Better Mousetraps well, of course, that's different. Our educational system, he continued, doesn't really know what business is all about and frankly doesn't want to know. Profit is still a dirty word. If your graduates came from a Redbrick, like Essex, or the LSE, then they'd probably been taught by a lot of long-haired yobbos who were no better than their pupils, and who encouraged them to kick down the front door, or set fire to the Dean. If you really want protest marches and demos, and all that sort of carry-on in your works what are the Trade Unions for, anyhow? If on the other hand your candidates had been to Oxbridge they'd probably been taught by dons who'd never been taught to teach, who insisted upon you learning Anglo-Saxon before you could take a degree in English, who revised their lectures once every seven years, only worked for six months out of the twelve, and spent the other six quarrelling bitchily with each other in the correspondence columns of *The New Statesman* and the *Spectator*. No, Mr. Chairman, sir—no university graduates in my business thank you.

A third year economics student from Christ Church put a different point of view. With some notable exceptions few British firms had a training policy worthy of the name. Even fewer, if they got hold of a graduate, took any trouble to find out what he had to offer, how his talents could best be used, or what further training he would be likely to need. A friend of his with a First in PPE had just got a job with a firm in the Potteries. On the first day at the factory they gave him a broom and told him to sweep out the works canteen. "I'm sorry," he said, "but that wasn't quite what I was taught to do at Oxford." "Right, lad," said the works manager, "chuck us that broom and I'll soon teach you how to do it." Couldn't a firm like that, asked Christ Church, do with a few protesters to shake them up a bit? And, in any case, profit *was* a dirty word. He and his friends were less interested in making money than they were in helping to put the world to rights. Had we seen "How to Succeed in Business Without Really Trying"? Business was indeed a nasty business. And what about take-overs and mergers? Look what happened to Joe Hyman and Cecil King—one was sacked for being too clever, and the other for not being clever enough. The armed services had their code—mutton-headed though it might be—the professions were governed by certain well-defined and accepted standards of conduct and the Civil Service was kept on the straight and narrow by the threat of a Parliamentary Question. But in business it was Devil take the hindermost, and this the Devil naturally did.

My summing up from the Chair pleased nobody, least of all myself. I don't think British management is anything like as bad as our Socialist friends, or our foreign competitors, are at pains to make out. Nor, however, do I think that we can afford to miss any opportunity of strengthening and improving our techniques. What the university graduate has to offer is not so much a knowledge of Anglo-Saxon as the advantages of a trained and disciplined mind. Many more such minds are now coming on to the market, and there are two obvious reasons for this. First, the brain drain has dwindled; few potential British drainees to the USA wished to be conscripted on to Vietnam. Secondly, we have now built about a dozen new Universities, though unfortunately we have built nothing like enough new teachers to man them. Too few of these trained minds however want to go into business despite a genuine effort by Government, universities and business itself to change this climate of opinion. Even though a firm like ICI may have 6,500 graduates on its books (though most of them are naturally chemists and scientists) there is still a prejudice against soiling one's hands in business, and this is nearly as deep rooted, and nearly as snobbish in its origin as it was when I myself was an undergraduate. When I was up at Oxford I had no thought of following my father in the boot and shoe trade. I went to the Bar instead. Amongst my close friends only Denis Greenhill was, as far as I can remember, destined for Commerce. He eventually joined the LNER but ended up as the distinguished head of our Diplomatic Service. Conversely, my poor old friend, Henry, who actually was destined for the Diplomatic Service, ended up by doing three years for fraudulent conversion in Rio de Janeiro. The rest of us thought nothing of business, if indeed we thought of anything except beer and blondes.

Oddly enough, the Americans are nearly as bad as we are at using intelligent men intelligently. Since the war only 12 per cent of their College Seniors, and fewer than 5 per cent of their Rhodes Scholars have elected to go into business.

Why are the Japs so much more kindly disposed to trade? Mr. Okomoto said that it was because the Americans take a man on for results, but the Japs take him on for life. The Japs never sack anyone for anything. To do so would involve a serious loss of face. So a boy can start thinking what firm he will join as soon as he is out of the nursery. This apparently is what does the trick. We Westerners, he thought, leave our indoctrination too late. And we must never forget the remarkable Japanese spirit of loyalty—loyalty to one's family, friends, firm, trade union, and loyalty, of course, to one's country. "Loyalty to one's University also?" I asked. "Yes, indeed, of course," replied Mr. Okomoto, as, beaming and bowing, he trotted out with more beer for the firemen.

# 22

# Business Expenses

"In Paris, it was Doris, the fairest of the
bunch,
But down in his expenses she was petrol,
oil and lunch".

And that, roughly, is what the expense account saga is all about.

Changes in the law have naturally brought forth some ingenious counter-moves. Before the war you took your secretary to Paris and called her your wife. (Early symptoms of a mistress have often been revealed by a sudden surge of creativity in an executive's expense account). Now, in order to wriggle through the tax-gatherer's net, you take your wife to Paris and call her your secretary.

The net had become little more than a series of loopholes tied together with red tape by the time the then Chancellor of the Exchequer thought up Sec. 15, ss. 4, of the Finance Act of 1965, the provisions of which you doubtless know by heart.

Mr. James Callaghan argued that there were, from time to time, circumstances in which a company's entertainment ought to be paid for out of the firm's profits, and not subsidised by the Exchequer. And he went on to suggest that too many businessmen made a habit of eating themselves daily into a stupor at the taxpayer's expense, and then drove nightly in the company car to the company's flat in preparation for their weekend on the company's salmon river or grouse moor.

I believe he did actually succeed in bringing one genuine company trout stream to light, but by and large Mr. Callaghan's picture was not only a travesty of the truth, but also a slander on the Inland Revenue who are usually down on this sort of thing like a duck on a June bug.

There may have been some abuse, not because the British businessman is basically dishonest, but because he regards the present level of taxation as confiscatory. He feels therefore that he is entitled to retain a bit more of the gravy, and to achieve this he occasionally oversteps the mark, and, alas, fudges his expenses.

Underlying all this, however, is a misapprehension of the whole concept of expense accounts, and this Mr. Callaghan and his friends, perhaps deliberately, did little to dispel. To begin with, few executives (by which I mean the sort of people who can take two hours off for lunch without being missed) have expense accounts at all. You have to take along to your company's accountant a record of what you have spent, and he invariably goes through this with a fine-tooth comb. "What's this," he cries, throwing up his hands in horror, "*two* chops for lunch? And after all that rich Spaghetti Bolognese you had with Mr. Midas at the Caprice on Monday. This will never do." (Incidentally, I believe the waiters in Rio de Janeiro make a fortune out of picking up receipted bills and selling them back at a profit in the appropriate quarter.)

The Act of 1965 produced further complications for our chief accountant; notably in the controversial person of the foreign buyer. His lunch, you will remember, remained chargeable to the Exchequer, whilst the native buyer's nosh had to be paid for by the company. This produced an awkward position if Mr. Mitsubishi from Kobe started off his lunch with you as a buyer, but eventually (deuced clever, these Orientals) ended up as a seller. It was more awkward still if you'd invited along some influential English friends to help impress your customer. "Come, Mr. Mitsubishi," you exclaim, "a little more of this excellent Mignon de Boeuf en Croute Lutece? And how do you find the Château Pichon-Longueville Baron '45? Just ready for drinking, don't you think? But how about you, Sir Basil, another sliver of the hake? And you, Hartley, a drop more of the Algerian, perhaps?".

This ludicrous arrangement had to be changed because it gave birth to the all-purpose notional foreign buyer. A machine tool firm of my acquaintance had a French director on their note paper. He didn't have to do much to earn his keep; he was the Chairman's nephew, and only held his job because of an interesting piece of boardroom blackmail. As soon as the 1965 Bill became law his colleagues changed him into a private company called Rentafrog, and then hired him out to any of their friends who wanted a tame foreigner to bring an export air to their luncheons. The scheme worked well enough for a while, but poor Alphonse had soon put on about two stone in weight, and was starting to develop cirrhosis of the liver. He eventually blew up one lunch time at the Ecu de France, and the whole scheme had to be recast.

It's easy, of course, to make fun of the "Who fed whom" announcements in *The Times*. Some business lunches are admittedly over-done, but at others a lot of genuine and important work is done as well.

The Americans call such luncheons eating meetings, but they have the uncomfortable habit of drinking neat gin before the meal, and freezing water with it. *Fortune Magazine*, however, recently revealed that a large number of important deals are in fact concluded over the luncheon table. Here in Britain such information is not so easy to come by. When the head-waiter at the Savoy Grill was asked how much business was discussed over lunch in the restaurant he replied coldly that it was not the job of the Savoy waiters to eavesdrop on their guests. My guess is that the situation is the same as in America.

In Japan the expense account has become a cross between a social accolade and a religion. If he gets black-balled for a fashionable expense account golf club the Japanese businessman commits hari-kiri. In Germany they try to get you tight over lunch so that you will tell them more about your p/e ratio than you intended. In Sweden businessmen spend three hours over lunch and tell very unbusiness-like stories. In other countries they have different habits, but few business communities can do without the practice in some form or other.

If Mr. Callaghan's Sec. 15 drove a lot of London restaurants out of business it may also have done a bit of good by stealth. Suppose your bright young executive, having spent his lunch break at Pruniers guzzling Pieds de Mouton Poulette washed down with the Gevrey Chambertin Lavany St. Jacques 1964, had to trot home in the evening to bangers and a bottle of Bass with the little woman in Godalming, he would notice the difference, and wouldn't like it. So the restrictions of Sec. 15 may have saved a few marriages although this advantage may have been offset by the rules about company flats. These desirable residences now have to be made available to all the directors of a company, and not just to one, otherwise the tax-gatherer will sting him for it as an emolument. An engineering firm we do business with in the Midlands accepted this point, and made appropriate changes in their company's arrangements. Unfortunately this wider use of the flat led to an outbreak of company wife-swapping, which was understandably mal-vu in Solihull. We must, however, be thankful for small mercies. At least Sec. 15 doesn't make us paint the name of our firm in bold letters down the side of the company car.

I hope that the present Chancellor of the Exchequer will take a long, hard look at the whole business. It's become messy, time consuming and undignified. I hope also that he will remember the extent to which an expense account has become, perhaps undesirably but none-the-less certainly, one of the perks attached to many responsible positions. Without it a lot of worthwhile people are going to find their jobs less rewarding, as well as more difficult. They will begin to think that the game is perhaps no longer worth the candle. Abolition of expense accounts could be in effect for them a vast increase in taxation. From time to time we hear about the brain drain. Unless the Chancellor gets to grips with this expense problem more realistically, even the stupid will begin to emigrate. The brainy, of course, will realise that the best way to remain solvent is to stay behind and live in sin, preferably with a girl who can cook.

# 23

# Women in business

MOST MEN have to wait until they are married in order to discover that women are just like other people. A less expensive way of finding this out is to work with them.

I've been fortunate to work with women in pretty well every job I've had, and I've never found them any trouble at all. It's the women who've never worked with men, and are never likely to, who make all the fuss.

The Labour Party came up with a Green Paper on "Discrimination against Women", and bless me if they didn't go and recommend that discrimination on grounds of sex should be made illegal, and an independent enforcement agency should be set up. As the whole point of Women's Lib. is to get women accepted on equal terms, there could hardly be anything more fatal than the creation of a special agency to defend feminine interests. You'd have all of us men shouting for the return to the straight and narrow path of kinder, küche, kirche in next to no time.

To my way of thinking, the chief trouble with women in business is that there aren't enough of them, and also, perhaps, that one or two of them occasionally want it both ways.

There are, in point of fact, very few jobs that are not yet open to women. They still, I believe, can't become Chairman of the Stock Exchange, or Archbishop of Canterbury, or Senior Steward of the Jockey Club or Mother Christmas. But give them time, give them time.

At my Prep school I was taught English and music by two splendid pin-cushiony ladies, and taught in such a way that I have retained a permanent affection for all four—English, music and the ladies. An English public school, however, is very different from a Prep school—or was. Roedean, one of our leading girls' schools, now has a headmaster, and most sensible this seems. Not many married women with children of their own have time to teach in school, and teaching is now very much a business. Elderly spinsters are not always ideally equipped to understand or encourage the teenage female mind. So more and more men now teach in girls' schools, and little harm seems to be done. But the teenager's brother still leads a hetero-sexual life for the four holiday months of the year, and a rigidly monastic life for the other eight. If I were a public school headmaster I'd see that at least twenty-five of my teachers were women. It would save a lot of trouble later on. But as some schools, and many university colleges are now going co-ed. this problem will gradually solve itself.

War is a business, too, and women, both in uniform and out, get dirty, and bombed, and killed, and win medals, too. I cherish one particular memory. After V.E. Day, up on the Dutch/German border we were suddenly turned into a mixed regiment. "Unbridled licence", our Padre wailed, "that's what we'll have." "Come, come," I said, "we've been going along as a regiment for seventy-five years without many cases of unbridled licence that I know of, even in Paddington, where we were raised. So why are we going to change our minds now"?

Well, of course, we didn't have any licence, unbridled or otherwise—or at least none that I got to hear about. All that happened was that the girls did a splendid job, the soldiery started to wash their hands before dinner, and their language improved out of all recognition.

Medicine is a business, too. I met a woman doctor professionally for the first time during the war in Prague when our jeep lost an argument with a coal truck. I only suffered a bent foot, and the good physician tied it up very nicely. But I couldn't help wondering how I should have liked it if the wound had been higher up. And then I remembered that most women have men doctors, and prefer it that way—so why was I being so prudish?

After the War I went back to work at the Bar. I shared a pupil room with a woman barrister who was also a champion golfer, and the only thing we quarrelled about was her ability to finish *The Times* crossword puzzle in ink before I had done half of it in pencil (you will gather that neither of us was over employed). The Law was one of the first trades to adopt a civilised attitude towards women, and we've had distinguished women magistrates, barristers and judges for years. When Mrs. Lane became our first female High Court Judge there was much debate, not about her qualifications, which were exemplary, but about her name. First, was she Mrs. Elizabeth Lane or Mrs. John Lane? And when she automatically became a Dame on reaching the Bench should she be addressed as Mr. Justice Lane, Madam or Mrs. Justice, My Lord, My Lady, or what have you? The pundits of Women's Lib. had a field day, and the Judge got on quietly with her job.

Although I think my chosen profession treated its ladies pretty courteously, the subject is always changed when the possibility of a Lady Chancellor crops up. Though the matter has never been resolved, it is also believed that neither a Jew nor a Roman Catholic can become Lord Chancellor because he is supposed to be the keeper of the Sovereign's (Protestant) conscience. So the authorities don't want a lady sending any more confusion swirling round the Woolsack. A lady can, of course, sit on the Woolsack as Deputy Speaker in the normal course of Parliamentary business, and Lady Wootton does so with much distinction.

We are, as a matter of fact, very fortunate with our Peeresses, and the gloomy and misogynist moanings that were heard at the time of their introduction have proved (with one exception) ill-founded. This exception was voiced by the late Lord Southampton who had a curly white beard, and looked like one of the statues come to life. "My lords," he exclaimed in the shortest speech of the debate, "It will play hell with the plumbing." And it did, too.

So much for the business of politics, from which I retired to find my way eventually into shipping. On the Board of Cunard sat Lady Tweedsmuir, and very good she was—so good, in fact, that H.M.G. soon prised her out, and appointed her to high Office.

My own experience of women in business has, therefore, been wholly agreeable. But I must confess that there is one type of woman who can be an infernal nuisance. She's the girl who won't admit that there's any difference between men and women in business, and insists upon men treating her like a man except, of course, when it suits her book to be treated otherwise. Sir Walter Raleigh laid his cloak in the puddle for Queen Elizabeth to walk on, and although she subsequently cut his head off, she approved of his behaviour at the time, and history has endorsed that approval.

Although this cloak and puddle stuff may be a bit strong by today's standards, the age of chivalry is not yet dead. Men still like to stand up when a woman enters the room, light her cigarette, open the door for her, and put her into the lifeboat before the captain and crew whenever possible.

We have recently been joined in the House of Lords by Lady Sharpe, who, as Dame Evelyn Sharpe was about the ablest Civil Servant with whom I ever had the privilege of working. I was scared stiff of her of course, but was happy to do her bidding. My predecessor (whose name was not actually Raleigh) told me that the best way to handle her was to bring her flowers, sit on her desk, and try to flirt with her. But I'm told you still got her way and not yours, though I never dared to try the ploy myself.

I'm all for women having equal rights in business, as in

everything else, but not equal privileges. They deserve and should be granted the greater privileges that are theirs by right of instinct, courtesy and tradition. And the few, the very few, who won't accept that situation should not be allowed in any self-respecting Boardroom. I have no objection to a business-woman using all the feminine tricks in the book, or out of it, because that's all part of the game. But Lord help them if they use tactics that would get a man kicked downstairs, and then burst into tears if anyone starts kicking them.

One last horror. No woman must ever call a man by his surname alone. Mr. Smith, fine. John, that's all right, too. But not just plain Smith—that's for men only. I'm sorry to say there's a certain Peeress who always calls me Mancroft, plain and simple. One day I'll retaliate, and call her a plain and simple name back—but it won't be hers.

# 24

# Taboo in business

WE'VE ALL now become so permissive that taboos themselves are almost taboo. Pornography, obscenity, nudity, illegitimacy, brawling in church, mugging your grandmother—you name it and you can have it.

There is, however, one place where taboos still flourish, and that, of course, is in business. And by business I don't just mean the City of London. I also mean business at its most business-like, from payola through to the Borough Council's building contracts, and thence to your Cayman Islands Bank account.

Time was when business itself was taboo. The eldest son looked after the estates, the second son went to the Bar, and the third (the simple one) went into the Army. The fourth, (the black sheep of the family) went into Business. He became something in the City, and this was not mentioned in polite society. It was, in fact, taboo.

It is only recently that business has become respectable and, more recently still, that the whizz-kids of commerce have achieved the heroic status they now enjoy. Dr. Johnson thought that even the most successful woollen-drapers were such wretches that no gentleman ought to pay them. And a glance through the back numbers of *Punch* will show you what Mr. Punch thought of the Victorian plutocrat. George du Maurier portrayed him as Sir Gorgias Midas, and the old brute was very taboo indeed. He was quite unreceivable in Society, a Society to which Mr. Punch also attributes a discreet touch of Anti-Semitism. (Nowadays, of course, Anti-Semitism has, itself, become taboo, at any rate in public.)

Both the horrible Sir Gorgias and some of today's Takeover Tycoons have hitherto shared one important taboo. They must never, but never, be found out. In the last few months, however, an embarrassing number of business men have not only been found out, but have actually volunteered to give some of it back. Now this will never do. Sir Gorgias must be turning in his grave, and even our own City Fathers have been nervously clearing their throats and explaining that one swallow doesn't make a summer; you mustn't judge the whole of the British business world by the fiddles of the few; in the City, a man's word is still his bond. And, anyhow, we've all had our doubts about the chairman of Consolidated Mulebreeders, even before the Sunday papers finally got on to him, and (privately) wasn't the Prime Minister a bit hasty with that remark about the unacceptable face of capitalism and won't that cause trouble at the back of the hall during the next General Election?

There are two schools of thought about the point at which a tut is tutted no longer and a taboo actually sets in. Some critics refer darkly to the tip of the iceberg. Many more people are now actively engaged in business. The gentleman who is today described as "assisting the police with their inquiries" was described in days gone by as unemployed or of no fixed abode. Now he is stated to be a company director. So both the tip and the iceberg are naturally bigger than they were.

It is not therefore quite true to say that today's businessmen are more dishonest than they were; it is simply that there are more of them to be found out. We must also remember that a taboo is not just something which is "prohibitive or under a ban". There is, says the O.E.D., a positive as well as a negative taboo. A taboo can also be something which has become consecrated, and it is when some brave fellow tries to deconsecrate it that the trouble really begins.

After forty years of splendid service, the faithful employee is usually presented with a gold watch and congratulated by the chairman upon his loyalty and devotion to duty. To these sentiments he makes appropriate reply. Not so, recently, one realistic toiler from Hitchin, Herts. As was widely reported at the time, he made quite a novel speech of thanks as he pocketed his watch. He told his employers how much and for how long he had despised them. He then went on to mention how boringly futile he had found his job, and how greatly he had looked forward to shaking the dust of their beastly factory from his feet.

This conduct imperils a very long consecrated taboo. What next, I ask?

The annual report of most company chairmen contains a ritualistic tribute to the staff, without whose loyalty, hard work, fine service, etc., etc., the profits, even when boosted by the pay freeze, could hardly have been attained.

Suppose a few chairmen, in their reports, should be tempted to edge a little nearer to the truth. Suppose one were to suggest that the staff were, in point of fact, a lot of lazy, dishonest and subversive layabouts. It was lucky there's been a bit of unemployment in the industry, because this has kept the incidence of strikes within manageable proportions. And if it hadn't been for the ever-increasing amount of pilferage throughout the works, profits would have been even bigger than they were.

And what about the Board? What about old General Twitterbottom, whose presence will be so greatly missed after forty-seven years wise counsel as a director, but who is now, at the age of eighty-eight, surely entitled to a little bit more leisure? Do we record the fuss he made when we plucked up courage and refused to grant him a third extension of office under Sec. 158 of the Companies Act? Is it taboo to remind the shareholders that he would never have got the job in the first place if he hadn't been the chairman's uncle; that the only business he ever brought to the company nearly landed us all in gaol and the only part of the accounts he could ever grasp was the bit about the directors' emoluments? No, of course we don't. Too much truth in business can also be taboo.

Some taboos are of more recent growth. To cast doubt, for instance, upon the necessity of employing the services of a merchant bank is frowned upon. Nor is it really wise to question the expertise of your business consultants, those ubiquitous gentlemen who are called in at the last moment to share the blame.

If a taboo is important in business, so also is the sanction against its infringement. In Bongoland, in days gone by, if you were rude to some important deity, you were probably roasted slowly over the fire. In Westminster, if you're found in bed with the wrong person you usually have to apply for the Chiltern Hundreds. But the standards of business are not so strict and sometimes the wrong person actually goes with the deal. But what happens in business if you're found, say, in the wrong prospectus? Precious little, I'm afraid.

People are judged not only by the company they keep but also by the company they keep away from. In business the line between illegality and unacceptability, between crime and taboo, is finely drawn. If you really break the law you may still go to gaol, always provided the Fraud Squad is not too overworked to notice. For doing what is only taboo, you hope to rely upon the shortness of people's memory, a widespread reluctance to kick up a fuss, or, worse still, a cynical belief that there really is nothing worse than being found out.

The Stock Exchange, Lloyds and the Baltic rightly pride themselves on the number of bargains that are still made on a man's word. There is a feeling that we should be more critical when such a word is broken. Too many rogues still get away with it. The rules of business are complex enough, in all conscience, but the general principles are pretty well understood. It is a pity there is not a sharper reaction when these rules are palpably bent.

I know that the days of duelling are over and some people

think this a pity. But surely there is still a little merit attaching to the cold shoulder, the ejection from the Club, the mantelpiece devoid of invitations?

For the more important bendings we have a new Companies Bill. This will no doubt help us to sort out the tips from the icebergs. I do hope, however, that it will at first not lay sacrilegious hands upon the sartorial taboos of business that happily still linger on.

The chairman of my bank tells me that his messenger will not let him go to see the Union Discount unless he wears a bowler hat. Hatlessness is apparently still taboo in the City of London, at least amongst its Senior Citizens. I am afraid that I do not myself possess a bowler hat but I am prepared to buy one if the chairman of my bank should ever wish me to call on him.

# 25

# Vanishing Britain

CHRISTMAS in times gone by was regarded as a religious festival, but this aspect now is scarcely apparent. Christmas is a huge commercial bonanza for the department stores, the bicarbonate of soda people, and the manufacturers of Christmas cards.

This Christmas you and I will display on our mantelpieces the usual quota of robins, wassail, yule-logs and snow-bejewelled holly. Most of the Christmasses I have been through have actually been snowless. More often than not they have been dank and slushy; just like any normal English summer day.

There are some who mourn the departure of the traditional Dickensian Christmas. Frankly, I don't believe it ever existed, and if it did I'm glad it's gone. Neither do I mourn the Victorian appetite that went with it.

My father was once the Lord Mayor of his native city of Norwich, and on the day of his election he gave the customary banquet. From the menu I have in my scrapbook it seems to have been sumptuous enough in all conscience. But it was a titchy little snack compared with what a predecessor of his had laid on some years before. That nosh was simply grotesque, and I can't think how they either got, or kept, it down. I suspect today's stomachs must have shrunk as a result of rationing in the war. How else can one explain those eighteen Victorian courses with wines to match, those herds of beef and flocks of sheep, those entrées and removes, and all those coneys and capons?

But outside the Banqueting Hall of St. Andrew's, even in a civilised city like Norwich, children were still crippled with rickets and T.B., the penalty for poaching was still seven years' penal servitude, young girls still worked indecent hours for a pittance, and respectable men and women died old, cold and starving in hovels in which you wouldn't nowadays put a pig. This also is a Britain that has vanished, and good riddance, too. Today you hardly ever see a down-and-out, or a waif and stray, or a beggar, or a drunken man in the streets, though this latter reform may have more to do with the price of gin than any serious improvement in drinking practices.

The slums of Britain are also vanishing (though slowly) but I'm not certain that I am really in love with the glass and concrete egg-boxes that are taking their place. Much fine agricultural land is also vanishing as the bull-dozers disembowel the countryside to make room for motorways. The new bypass is to come a mile from our village; the noise and the smell will be hideous, but I'm told that we shall once again be able to walk in the streets without being squashed by a 40-foot container. This will be nice. We are also told that because of our accessibility to London the price of our property will appreciate, and this will also be nice.

The river flows through the bottom of our garden, except in the months of January and February when it flows through the kitchen, Nanny's bedroom, and the larder. It's a pretty little river, but, like so many others, it is in danger of vanishing under a surge of detergents, just as the view of the Cotswolds from my bedroom window has vanished behind a cat's-cradle of pylons. Behind them lies Fairford, the home of the Concorde, which drops in on us from time to time. Heaven help our greenhouse roof if the pilot really decides to get a move on, because a man who can repair a greenhouse roof is another significant feature of vanishing Britain. He is going the same way as thatchers, wheelwrights, hurdle-makers, blacksmiths, and the publican who can bother to keep draught beer.

A pair of hands is the most expensive thing in this country today, and service is something that has vanished more noticeably than anything else. I'm not just referring to the difficulty of finding a good second footman. I'm thinking of the difficulty of getting a clock repaired, or the groceries delivered, or of finding a garage that can overhaul your car in such a way that the last state of that car will not be worse than the first.

Whence, I ask, has everybody gone? The Armed Services and the Police are desperately short of recruits, you can't get a good shorthand-typist for love or money, you have to queue for hours to get served in a shop even if you are not asking for something that is out of stock, trains are always being cancelled because of a lack of drivers, and most of the hospitals in the country would grind to a halt if it weren't for all those cheerful little West Indian nurses.

Well, I'll tell you where everybody has gone. We're simply doing the same jobs that half the number of people did more efficiently before the war. We're clamouring for a four-day week. In point of fact we've already got it; it's just that we need five days in which to do the job. We're no longer interested in giving service because service is now regarded as degrading, and too redolent of the touched forelock. Well done, thou good and faithful servant? Sometimes, but not often.

What people now demand is more leisure. As I'm in the leisure business myself I suppose I shouldn't grumble. And watching the crowds of visitors enjoying their leisure at the Changing of the Guard you realise that pageantry happily plays no part in vanishing Britain. There are some who maintain that to concentrate too much on the Opening of Parliament, the Tournament, Stratford, the Crown Jewels, Mrs. Wilson's poetry, and all the rest of the British Tourist Authority's stock in trade gives foreigners a distorted image of the country. Maybe—but it's the Changing of the Guard that the visitors come to see. They are not really interested in nuclear reactors, Redbrick University, or the Milk Marketing Board. Nor, frankly, am I. But I think there's something more to pageantry than the money it brings in from the tourists. It's part of the national character.

A lot of Britain that has vanished would never have gone if people had not been greedy, thoughtless, or just plain daft. But a lot of rubbish has vanished, too. On reflection the balance sheet doesn't really look so bad. I'm sorry that Nash's Regent Street, and Baronetcies, the Grand Jury, Ally Pally and Ealing films have all vanished, but I don't mind so much about the loss of bear-baiting, the slave trade, and public executions, all of which were much appreciated in their time. I think that some of our nostalgia for what has vanished is misconceived. Nothing is so flattering to the Good Old Days as a Bad Old Memory.

And, with all its faults, Britain is still one of the most beautiful countries in the world, and its people amongst the kindest and most honest.

# 26

# Souvenirs

I THINK that the American gentleman who bought London Bridge as a souvenir and plonked it down in the middle of Arizona had all the right ideas. And London Bridge has all the right qualifications for the perfect souvenir. It is handsome, it is unusual, and since there appears to be no water in Arizona it is also completely useless.

Indeed, I can only think of one other souvenir in the same class, and that was the baby alligator which was given to my Uncle Eustace as he was leaving a party of Bright Young Things in the spring of 1927. He took it home to his flat in Albany and put it in the bath. Next morning the alligator was still there, though looking understandably peaky. My Uncle's man-servant, however, had gone, leaving a note on the kitchen dresser. "Sir," it read, "I cannot work for a gentleman who keeps baby alligators in his bath. I would have mentioned this when you engaged me but I never thought it was likely to arise."

Into the more orthodox class of souvenir there falls a wide range of plastic Guardsmen, sticky pink rock with "Blackpool" written all through, and delicately-wrought dolls' tea-sets proclaiming that they are a present from Budleigh Salterton. About all such items there have been complaints both as to suitability and as to design.

Ever vigilant, the Council of Industrial Design mounted an exhibition which demonstrated convincingly that it's just as easy to design a good-looking plastic Guardsman as a bad one. The Council, however, did not convince everybody that a plastic Guardsman, even if designed by Lord Snowdon himself, is what we really want. Is this the image of the dynamic, pragmatic, gritty, nuclear-orientated Britain that we would like our visitors to take home and display on the mantelpieces of Kimberley and Kalamazoo?

Well, it may not be what *we* want, but unfortunately it appears to be what the tourists want. You try selling them scale model manganese gudgeon sprockets or elegantly framed mezzotints of Didcot power station, and see where that gets you.

We're expecting 15 per cent more tourists this year than last; and it therefore looks as if London in August is going to contain more tourists than natives. There's even talk of Changing the Guard twice daily. I personally am against this. It is, after all, the Palace and not the Palladium. But is any enterprising coach operator planning package tours to sunny Harwell, or arranging escorted outings to Guest, Keen & Nettlefolds? I think not. It'll be the same old circuit as ever; the Crown Jewels and Stratford, Windermere and Windsor Castle, and Laurence Olivier if anyone can fiddle some tickets. And why not? That's the state of the market. That's what our visitors come for, and its models of the Crown Jewels and their guardian Beefeaters (sorry, Yeomen Warders) that they'll want to take home, not to mention tea-cloths with pictures of the Tower and (if they know the right shop in the Kings Road) ladies' frilly garters with the Royal Borough's Coat of Arms embroidered on one side and "Fix thy thoughts on things above" on the other. (The same emporium used to sell knickers made out of the Stars and Stripes until the American Embassy protested, and quite right too.)

On the other hand I suspect that the progress of science must be making serious inroads into these branches of the souvenir trade. Amateur photography has now become more professional than can be good for the future of the postcard industry. A stereo record of Trooping the Colour brings back more vivid memories than a thousand plastic Guardsmen. The tape recorder is also here to stay. When *QE2* passed the old *Elizabeth* lying stricken off Aruba, the two ships exchanged greetings and the short recording we made of their reunion is almost painfully evocative.

Perhaps science can help us further still. I was telling you about my Uncle Eustace. Well, he eventually steadied up and married Auntie Hetty who survived him by many years. On the end of her drawing-room sofa she kept a little rubber air cushion upon which nobody was allowed to bounce. We children always understood that it contained poor Uncle's dying breath. Now here's the germ of a useful idea. Before the Six-days War the Israelis used to do a lively trade in bottled Jordan water. So what about bottled Heathrow fog, or dehydrated Centre Court rain pills to be reactivated when you return to Tallahassie, Fla., and want to describe your European trip to all the lovely people back home?

The trouble is, of course, that the souvenirs we would really like our visitors to take home are always the most difficult to put together. I live in a small village in the Cotswolds. This weekend we've had an American friend to stay, and the weather's been really lovely. This is just as well because the last time he was over the weather was vile and he went home complaining that the English base their domestic heating arrangements on an exaggerated confidence in the Almighty, the Gulf Stream and two small lumps of Coalite.

Last Sunday, however, restored his faith in the English climate. The cherry blossom was at its best, the cuckoo was shouting its silly head off, and the bees were about their business. The church tower was solid gold in the morning sunlight. Our guest sat under the lilac on the lawn drinking Pimms No. 1, on the composition of which I had just delivered a scholarly teach-in. "This is it," he said, sweeping his arm round our garden, "I'll take all this back as a souvenir. Wrap it up for me at once. Never mind your plastic Guardsmen. You can keep your Anne Hathaway Cottage tea-cosies. Away with your phallic glass tubes of Alum Bay coloured sand. Just wrap this all up for me and I'll take it back to Chicago." "Very good, Sir," I replied, "and would there be anything else?"

He paused reflectively. "Yes," he said, "there is. You can slip in Princess Anne, Marks & Spencer, and Question Time in the House of Commons."

I must see what I can do.

# 27

# Kicking up a fuss

THERE SEEMS to be a revival in the art of kicking up a fuss, and this is all to the good. During the last railway strike Osbert Lancaster's strike-bound Dowager inquired indignantly to what rule the engine-driver thought he was working, and, in real life, endlessly delayed commuters thumped the railway men who were making their lives a misery. The commuters' action may have been unseemly, but the principle is sound. The worm who has forgotten how to turn is brushing up his rotation drill.

His forebears turned more readily. The Fourth Earl of Cringleford, dissatisfied with the apology proffered by a hansom-cab driver who had short-changed him outside White's, so laboured him with his ivory-handled cane that the wretched fellow dropped senseless from his seat. This behaviour was considered rough even by the standards of White's, and the committee requested his lordship, if he felt minded to repeat the performance, to do so outside Pratt's.

How often today do we even bother to count our change, let alone remonstrate with the taxi-driver? It could be that we are so overjoyed at actually having found a taxi that we are rendered speechless, but if it is only that we have left our ivory-handled cane at home, why don't we just withold the tip?

Mr. Ritz, the hotelier, tells us in his memoirs of a Parisian customer who, finding something amiss with his soup, summoned the chef, and poured the whole plate over him. What diner-out today would even dare to send a dish back, let alone resort to culinary violence?

If you take your faulty electric kettle back to the shop you know in advance what will happen. If they eventually admit that you did buy it there they will tell you that yours is the first complaint they've ever received, and in any case they don't undertake repairs.

So it is with your new car. Complain to the manufacturers that thirty-seven pieces have fallen off since you bought it ten days ago; ask whether their products could not be slightly inspected before leaving the assembly line, and you will be told that such a demand would only result in a strike—it would constitute a reflection on the workers.

If you successfully challenge your telephone bill you will be told that it is all the fault of the computer. Pluck up courage and remind them that if they put rubbish into one end of a computer rubbish will come out at the other, and your phone will be cut off at once.

Is this, then, why we so seldom pluck up our courage? Is this why the worm so infrequently turns? Have we really become so sensitive that we shrink from any public display of disapproval? During the war we put up with snoek and powdered eggs, and considered ourselves lucky to get them. Have our critical powers now become irretrievably blunted? To complain about anything in 1943 was tantamount to treason. Is it, in 1973, only a fatalistic recognition of the current laws of supply and demand? And has our distaste for hijacking and burnt Embassies, protest marches and student demos soured our taste for the personal demo, however cold the soup, or short the change?

A few static worms may think of a simpler answer. Life today has become so complex, our social structures so involved, and our commercial connections so impersonal that it seems the all-powerful "they" will always beat the helpless you and me. What avails it to complain about the rent, or the leaking roof, if your landlord's identity changes every week? Why bother to grumble to the local Fuel Office if your letters are not answered (the computer is perhaps on leave) and your phone calls never returned? If the County Council are determined to drive a new road through your sitting-room they'll drive it—so save your breath, and start to look for a new home now.

Mr. Harold Wilson, of all people, has been drawing attention to the harm the "grey they" can do. Right, of course, is on his side, but to those who can remember which political party once maintained that the Gentleman in Whitehall knew best, a raised eyebrow may not be out of order.

The trouble is that the Gentleman in Whitehall often does know best. We wouldn't mind so much if only he would give his reasons. Of course the engine-driver has the right to withhold his labour, but surely not to work to rules which a reasonable man finds fatuous, and the observance of which hurts the maim, the halt and the blind. Of course bills must ultimately be paid, but surely we haven't yet lost the right to check them? What we should seek is not just a more powerful Ombudsman, but a more mobile worm.

The battle of Crichel Down ended in two famous victories. We re-established the standards of honour by which a Minister of the Crown ought still to be judged. We established, too, the principle that the citizen is entitled to have his affairs handled not only with justice, speed and efficiency, but also with due regard to his personal feelings. These sentiments, said *The Times*, in its leading article, should hang enframed above the desk of every public servant. Well, let's see. Worms of the World Unite—you have nothing to lose but your red tape!

Allow me to give a lead. Next week I am engaged to see my tax-gatherer, and woe betide him if the lesson of Crichel Down is not hanging over his desk for all to see. Incidentally, I shall take with me not only the relevant files and correspondence, but my ivory-handled cane as well.

# 28

# Some people enjoy flying

THERE ARE, I believe, some people who actually enjoy flying.

I myself prefer to travel by sea, and I preferred to travel by sea even before I went to work for a shipping company. Time, however, compels and if you have to cross the Atlantic about six or seven times a year and wish to see your office and your home from time to time, you must occasionally travel by air. And if you travel by air you must inevitably end up at an airport, and all airports are hell, and few people want to come home via hell.

Southampton Docks, I admit, lack chic. Pier 92 at New York obviously has its admirers, but I am not among them. And however eager one is to return home there are still faults to be found with the Customs Shed at Tilbury, the Immigration pen at Liverpool, and the toilet facilities in the Royal Docks. All, however, are to be preferred to any airport anywhere.

Let me, nevertheless, be fair. Let me examine just one airport, LAP (or Heathrow—they can never make up their minds what to call the wretched place), in ideal circumstances. As far as I am concerned, the last time these circumstances occurred was at the end of a journey home from America on Wednesday, the 17th ult. Everything had gone unusually well. At JFK (or

Idlewild--they can never make up their minds what to call the wretched place) my connecting aircraft had arrived on time from California. There had been no stacking, none of the aeronautical ritual dance that lasts for hours whilst they shoo a Piper Cub off the runway, or lure the traffic controller back from the coffee shop. The Departure Lounge, where pandemonium usually reigns, was quiet. I discount the inevitable flock of nuns fluttering anxiously to and fro, since they are to be found at every airport. I've met them as far afield as Bembridge, Bahrein and Tuscaloosa. For all I know it may be the same flock of nuns going round and round and provided by the Vatican in the way that the Brigade of Guards provide the Stage Army for *Aïda* at Covent Garden.

Over the public address system came a message that for once I understood. Usually such announcements begin with the words "Ug, glug, snumph" but this particular message informed us clearly that our aircraft was now ready for boarding at Gate 4 and this Gate, to my relief, proved to be straight ahead instead of the usual seventeen miles to the north-east.

The weather was superb. Tuesday was one of New York's rare fog-free days (I often wonder how the Americans dare breathe a word of criticism about London). Although our pilot had warned us that we might encounter "a considerable amount of slight turbulence", everything turned out well and the journey was uneventful. My neighbour, whose baggage tag proclaimed him as returning from Hong Kong, bade me a civil good day and remained silent for the rest of the trip. On my last journey in the States I had sat next to an articulate lady who told me that she contributed the daily gossip column to her local newspaper; she also told me what she had written in the previous seven editions, and what she proposed to write in the next fourteen. (This sort of thing does not happen in Ships.) So I liked the quiet look of the gentleman from Hong Kong.

The food was edible. I sometimes wonder why airlines don't worry less about their complimentary boutonnières and their free bottles of scent, and worry more about the food. I believe, however, that there are international regulations which discourage this. Anyway, the food was edible and the Bloody Marys potable. They were made for us by our friendly Hostess, Eloise, whose measurements were apparently 36-25-36. I need hardly say that I had not myself raised this matter but some wag up front had scribbled the information on the track chart.

My neighbour was not only silent, he was also stationary. I usually find myself sitting next to nomadic types who roam around the cabin just as I am nodding off to sleep.

Thanks to the immobility of my neighbour from Hong Kong I slept soundly. In next to no time we were slipping down over Uxbridge, which is not among our prettiest towns but which was shimmering pleasantly in the morning sun. Furthermore, Uxbridge is in England and one Englishman at least was happy to be home.

Normally my ears pop for two days after a Transatlantic flight, but our pilot had the hands of a Rubinstein. Customs and Immigration were no less smooth and our baggage was handled swiftly. My car was waiting for me, and whilst my cases were being loaded by an unusually polite porter I strolled over to an empty phone box which I was surprised to find in working order. I got through at once to my wife and found all well at home.

I left the box wondering how the phone system would work in Manchester when a couple of Jumbo-jets are simultaneously diverted from LAP, and a crowd about the size of the population of Malmesbury all try to ring their homes at the same time. I dismissed this thought and considered how lucky I had been on this particular trip. For once nothing had gone wrong. No frustrations of time and tide (which defeat us today as thoroughly as they defeated the pre-computerised Canute), no unforeseeable piece of bad luck, no incompetence of my own or of the airline, nor any bloodymindedness of the TUC's two and seventy jarring sects had upset my home-coming as they had so often done before.

I was smiling smugly to myself when I noticed my friend

from Hong Kong emerging from the next door phone box. His face was black as thunder. I broke our Trappist silence and asked if anything was amiss. There was. He had telephoned his flat and, unlike me, had received no welcoming reply. He had then telephoned his secretary and was told Yes, indeed, they had received his telegram and yes, indeed, they were expecting him home but not, indeed, today. A great light suddenly dawned on him. He had mis-interpreted the International Date Line and had given his family the wrong date.

I went over to the bar and bought myself a pint of bitter. This you can still do at LAP, though probably not for much longer. Draught bitter will become Keg, and the LAP licensing laws will become those of Uxbridge. As I drank I noted how much better English beer tastes than the gloriously golden, gassy, frozen nothing which they have the audacity to call beer in the USA. I also noted that there is something not altogether displeasing to us in watching the misfortunes of others.

# 29

# Talking shop

IMMEDIATELY AFTER last Christmas one of the junk-shops in the Kings Road put up a notice in the window warning us that there were only 292 shopping days till Christmas. The proprietor amended the figure daily, but many people went in to question his mathematics. He put their minds at rest by reminding them that not only was he closed on Sundays, but also (which they had probably not appreciated) on Yom Kippur, and the beginning of Ramadan as well, out of consideration for the international nature of his clientèle. His would-be critics were satisfied by this explanation and left, often as not, clutching a useful hat-stand or elegantly decorated papier-mâché tea-caddy. The proprietor was a salesman as well as a psychologist.

In refined places like the Kings Road, Bond Street and Beaumont Place, the boutique and the junk-shop can still hold their own, but little shops elsewhere are steadily being crowded out by the supermarkets and the do-it-yourself emporia. Here, I realise, psychology and salesmanship are also needed, but of a different kind. For my part I have had a guilt-complex about supermarkets ever since the occasion when I reached up for a tin of tomato purée and accidentally pulled down the whole pyramid. It crashed around my ears with a noise like Tchaikovsky's 1812 Overture, and the tins bounced far and wide. Two little Jamaican assistants ran to my rescue, and untinned me. They were quite nice about it but clearly indicated that in future I oughtn't to be allowed to go shopping without Nanny. Actually I suspect that Nanny would have been as terrified as I am of the supermarket's soulless, but not always selfless, efficiency! (2p off! Great bargain! But off what?)

Nanny's favourite shop was Gaylor & Pope, then in Marylebone High Street, and now replaced by a Woolworth's. An obsequious shop-walker would glide towards you in a beautiful morning coat, and bow politely from the waist. Trim little shop-assistants asked if they could help you, Moddom. Too many of their counterparts today, if you ever succeed in diverting their attention from their manicure or crossword puzzle, make it only too clear that your request for service is an unwarrantable invasion of their privacy.

But the real glory of Gaylor & Pope was the overhead railway which whisked a ball containing your bill and money along to the counting-house high up in the centre of the shop. Here, at the seat of custom, sat Miss Gaylor herself. I can see her now, a podgy little figure in black bombazine, with fluffy grey hair, and large round specs, looking not unlike Lord George-Brown in drag. She was never once known to make a mistake with the change, and if your ribbons came to 3s. 11¾d. you didn't get a farthing back from your 4s. as change—you got a packet of pins instead. And she gave us mint humbugs when Nanny's back was turned.

I know all about the immense range and variety offered to you by the supermarkets of today, but I miss Gaylor & Pope as much as I shall miss the little village shops of my childhood. These, also, seem to be doomed.

My parents used to take a house at Cromer for the holidays, and our corner shop was run by old Mrs. Thirkettle, who was generally believed to be a witch. Her familiar was a leery black tom named Nebuchadnezzar, who dozed peacefully on a sack of lentils but sprang to instant and spitting life if anyone ever tried to buy lentils. Mrs. Thirkettle sold everything you could imagine, and we used to put her to the test by running round with demands for a pint of turps, two dozen liquorice all-sorts, a ball of twine, some curling tongs and yesterday's *Eastern Daily Press*. She soon realised we were having her on, and used to chase us from the shop, flailing us with a wet dish-cloth.

It looks as if departmental stores are on the way out too. They will also be missed, particularly at Christmas. There are still, of course, people who look upon Christmas as a particularly charming religious festival, but there are others who regard it as a huge commercial spree, a chance to recoup from the losses inflicted upon the High Street by a disastrously wet August, or a power strike. No opportunities must be missed. Round about October the maintenance men descend upon the fancy goods department, or floor coverings, or men's shirtings (Gaylor & Pope used to call an evening shirt a "gent's stiff half-bosom") and heave the whole lot out. In next to no time the area is transported into Santa's Grotto, and Father Christmas moves in.

They're an interesting body of men, those rubicund old chaps who sit out the day perspiring under their whiskers and exuding an aroma which the children are led to believe comes from grooming reindeer, but is actually attributable to Hammerton's Oatmeal Stout. They dish out rather undistinguished presents to those children who have blackmailed their parents into buying tickets. The blackmail can, however, work both ways. One Santa of my acquaintance, who used to work in the summer as a bouncer at a Blackpool amusement arcade, was once nearly caught by a little curly-haired darling who whispered in his ear as she climbed onto his knee to receive her present that if he didn't slip her a quid at once she would tell her mother that he had tried to do something beastly. I'm glad to report that the little C.H.D. and her mama (who was, of course, in the act) were ejected with less than the usual Christmas spirit, and a word of warning to other stores was passed round by the Santa's union.

In America they are not so grotto-minded as we are. In New

York the Santas walk up and down the pavement ringing bells and ho-ho-hoing for all they're worth. Aromatically they lean towards Rye-on-the-Rocks rather than Oatmeal Stout. And I'm sorry to have to admit it, but the shop windows outside which they patrol are better dressed than ours. London's windows, and a few perhaps in Edinburgh, are good. I give the prize to Burberrys, even though I must confess I used to be their deputy chairman.

British shop windows are on the whole better than most on the Continent, but they lack the flair and panache of the shops on Fifth Avenue, in San Francisco and Palm Beach. Of course, it is only fair to admit that they lack also American purchasing power. Fortnums, Aspreys, and Garrards are not places for paupers, but even those Aladdin's caves are hard put to it to challenge the opulence of a store like Tiffanys in New York, or the brash virtuosity of Neiman-Marcus in Dallas, which specialises in presents for the man (or woman) who has everything. The last time I was there, the local cinemas were showing "Cleopatra", and Neiman-Marcus naturally was selling asses' milk.

Harrods, I believe, still boast that they sell everything from a harmonium to a hamster, and greatly though I admire Mr. Stanley Marcus (on whom the landing space for flies is small) I don't believe that even his store offers to do quite as well as that.

# 30

# In defence of patriotism

WHEN WE find Dr. Johnson and George Bernard Shaw in agreement there must surely be something amiss.

Johnson thought Patriotism was the last refuge of a scoundrel, and has thereby puzzled us ever since. Boswell tried to help by prefacing his report with the warning that Johnson "suddenly uttered an apothegm at which many will start". You bet they will! My own view is that Johnson didn't really mean patriotism at all. He was either referring to nationalism of which (with the disturbing manifestations along the Potomac in mind) he clearly did not approve, or else the old boy was tight. In any case it only goes to show that among the many things that can be done to an apothegm it should never be suddenly uttered. Cries can be suddenly uttered, yes; exclamations, certainly; but not apothegms.

GBS went even further; he said that we should never have a quiet world until we threw patriotism out of the human race. He, too, was probably thinking of nationalism, if, indeed, he had given the matter any serious thought at all.

Bismarck, of all people, probably got nearer to the difference between the two concepts when he refused a glass of German champagne on the grounds that his patriotism stopped short of his stomach. I wonder, however, how he regarded the views of the Austrian dramatist, Grillparzer, who argued that the path of modern culture leads from humanity through nationality to bestiality. In seeking, therefore, to defend one's own patriotism one must be careful not to defend nationalism at the same time.

And why not? Well, too many Democrats and Totalitarians; Liberals and Conservatives; Marxists and Fascists, and many other adherents to a wide variety of political creeds have, since the eighteenth century, all found the doctrine of nationalism an adaptable, readily available and potent weapon. Alas, many still do. If, however, we regard patriotism as the love of our own country, and nationalism the dislike of somebody else's, we're going to have difficulty in explaining our own British brand of xenophobia.

Coloureds (sorry, Afro-Asians) were always supposed to begin at Calais, and if there was a bad fog in the Channel we were told that the Continent was isolated. "Who's that?" asked Mr. Punch's working man in the 1870's. "Dunno," replies his friend, "must be a stranger." "Right, 'eave 'alf a brick at 'im." I doubt if that was an accurate picture of Britain then, and I hope it isn't now. But leaving aside a suspicion of all foreigners which is one of the few things that unites the British people, and is at the back of all our doubts about the Common Market. I don't really believe there's any such animal as a true British patriot. Scottish, Irish and Welsh, of course. Ulster, Cornwall and Yorkshire, too; and don't let us forget Home Rule for the Isle of Man. But I'm not too sure about British patriotism as a genus on its own.

By the way, did anyone mention the English? Well, I do, and in the Queen's English rather than the Queen's British. I haven't a drop of anything except English blood in my veins, and it always seems to me that when pride of ancestry is being vaunted we English get the dirty end of the stick. Nobody remembers us at all. We're hidden behind the Celtic fringe. That's why I always put down "English", rather than "British" on an immigration form.

Please don't think I've got anything against the Scots. Far

from it. They're a splendid people—world beaters. I can even accept the romantic but commercially rewarding brand of patriotism they've been manufacturing for so long. They have every reason to be proud of Walter Scott, shortcake, bagpipes and Edinburgh Rock, of Export regiments like the Toronto Scottish, the Transvaal Scottish, and, for all I know, the Wagga Wagga Scottish, too. I once went to a Burns Night dinner in Singapore, where we ate about a hundredweight of haggis, which Dr. Johnson called fine confused feeding; and at ninety degrees in the shade it can be very confused feeding indeed. This sort of patriotism is really no more than a realistic home-sickness. It's charming, and it must bring tears of pride to exiled Highland eyes to see a whisky advertised in Ceylon as being "made from genuine Scottish grapes". But when the Scots turn from harmlessly slapping their own backs, when they turn from patriotism to nationalism and start blowing up letter-boxes because they are inscribed QIIE, then they are not quite so charming.

So it is with the Welsh, whom I also love. I admit that I have never been able to keep a straight face at an Eisteddfod, but their language is lovely, and they are right to fight like tigers for its survival. I do wish, however, they hadn't gone so far as to insist upon English-speaking Welsh children having to learn the language, too. And I don't like the Welsh National Army, at all.

There are, of course, those who favour Home Rule for Wales and Scotland because this would result in a permanent Socialist government in Cardiff and Edinburgh (which would serve them all right) and a permanent Tory government in London (which would be nice). I don't know what would happen in the Isle of Man, and I don't think I am going to try to find out, because it's when you start to mix patriotism with politics that trouble really begins.

I used to be Chancellor of the Primrose League, and at our annual hooley (which we camouflaged with the splendid title of Grand Habitation) we always sang Land of Hope and Glory

—and more than one verse, too. When I first joined the League we were enjoying potato rationing and Sir Stafford Cripps, a situation which was neither very glorious nor gave much ground for hope. But although matters eventually improved I've always been a bit uneasy about the sentiments of L of H & G, staunch Tory though I am. I'm also uneasy about our Party's habit of pinning the Union Jack on the chairman's table at political meetings. Oddly enough the point cropped up this very election-tide. A questioner rose up at the back of the hut, and asked why we did it. "Because," said our man, "the Conservative Party is the patriotic Party." The questioner did not appear to be satisfied. "Are you suggesting," he inquired, "that the eleven million or so who will vote Socialist on Thursday are all traitors?" "No," said our man, "but I am stating, and not just suggesting, that your Party once sang The Red Flag in the House of Commons, and far too many of your Members insult the Americans, who are our friends, and actively support the Russians, who wish us ill. Next question please." All thirty-seven persons present seemed satisfied, and we passed on to problems of the eleven-plus, and the price of lettuces.

I think most of us are patriotic in differing ways. Scotsmen, Manxmen and what-you-will men, we're all proud of Canterbury Cathedral, and the Bill of Rights, Hamlet and Marks & Spencer. We also have our private mini-patriotisms like the Chelsea Flower Show, or the Eton Boating Song, Rolls-Royce, Guinness and the Arsenal. We thought of these things nostalgically when we were queueing up on the beaches at Dunkirk, and we think of them again if we find ourselves stationed in China or Peru. Patriotism helps to keep our morale out of the mud.

In America respect for The Stars and Stripes provides for a polyglot nation a good patriotic focal point. (The Israelis have found the same use for the Hebrew tongue.) We take the Union Jack more light-heartedly.

Basically our patriotism is directed less to the Flag than to the Throne, and despite the distrust of people like Aneurin Bevan for what he called the "ballyhoo of Buck House", this country remains profoundly Royalist, and for two very good reasons. The Monarchy suits us, and it works. Any other form of patriotism that can pass this test is acceptable. If it doesn't it's probably nationalism, and suspect.

What a Nairobi-born Pakistani waiter, working in Llandudno, and married to an Irish chambermaid from Glasgow, would make of an Eisteddfod is, of course, a slightly different problem.

# 31

# Statuesque

I DON'T know who was the model for Epstein's statue of Rima in Hyde Park, but my grandmother thought nothing of her at all. "Dammit," the old lady remarked as we were passing by on our Sunday stroll, "I'm nearly eighty myself, but if I couldn't strip off better than that, I'd cut my throat."

Most people, however, do know that the model for the statue of "Justice" which used to stand to the left of Queen Victoria in the House of Lords was the Mistress of the Robes, and the model for the statue of "Mercy" on the right was the mistress of the sculptor.

I myself, though this is not yet generally known, have also been in the business. I was the model for three inches of Winston Churchill's right trouser leg on the Oscar Nemon statue in the House of Commons. I happened to be in Mr. Nemon's studio one morning when he was having a little trouble with the hang of Winston's trousers, and he asked if I would oblige by posing for a few minutes. Bursting with pride I obliged, and have thereby passed into history.

But Winston's statue, grand as it is, has already given rise to controversy. My bit of trouser is on a level with Lloyd George's coat button on the opposite side of the Arch, and the Welsh Liberals don't approve of Winston towering over their hero.

However much the pigeons may regret it, I am beginning to wonder whether the day of the statue isn't over. A statue, even one like that of Alderman Rufflebottom's in front of the local Corn Exchange, must be cast in the heroic mould, and the days of heroics are drawing to a close. Look at Nelson in Trafalgar Square. Splendid! But is anyone seriously thinking of a similar carry-on for Monty, or Alex, or Admiral Cunningham? And in any case, if you'd taken a vote in 255 Battery RA, you'd have been told that their real war hero was the chap who invented self-heating soup. A couple of tins of that elixir might make an interesting subject for Henry Moore, or Anthony Caro, but the result would give rise to debate, and somebody would be sure to come along and daub it with red paint, or better still try to blow it up.

That's the trouble with statues; they're like Embassies, provocative. Next time you're in Winchester Cathedral, have a look at the gaudy statuette of Joan of Arc up by the Lady Chapel. It wasn't until it had been unveiled, and the notables had said their pieces and departed that someone noticed that the Maid had been put looking straight into the tomb of Cardinal Beaufort, one of the men who had voted her on to the stake. Understandably, there was trouble; mutterings in the Close, narky letters in the *South Hants Advertiser* and so on.

Statues are now becoming even more controversial, and this worries me. Easily though I am able to contain my admiration for Karl Marx, I wasn't pleased when they recently blew up the old brute's bust in Highgate Cemetery. What next, I asked myself? If the Comrades don't get proper satisfaction they'll have Disraeli off his plinth in next to no time. Then somebody will take a long hard look at the statues in the curtilage of the Palace of Westminster; there are only two of them, and they are, oddly enough, of Oliver Cromwell, who tried to abolish Parliament, and Richard the First, who never summoned it. So the King Charles Society will try and heave Old Noll into the Thames, and the United Arab League (mindful of the Crusades) will put a bomb under R. Coeur de Lion. Then we shall really be down to basics and somebody will turn up the record and find out all about the row that Alderman Rufflebottom had with the Safeblowers Union in March of 1886, and the Corn Exchange will be in for trouble too.

Foreigners arrange these things more calmly. The Indians, for instance, pull the statues of British generals and governors from their plinths with a gentle Oriental decorum. For my taste, however, they recently went too far. At the very moment they were hauling some viceroy off his horse in Bombay, they were asking us to subscribe to the erection of a statue to Gandhi in Bloomsbury Square.

Come to think of it, what are the Indians actually doing with all our generals and governors once they have got them down? Are they storing them in a Generals' and Governors' Museum, as the GWR have done with the Cheltenham Flyer and its mates in the Railway Museum at Swindon? And are they planting their horses and elephants out in the open like the dinosaurs and pterodactyls that used to mope around the Crystal Palace before we burnt it down? I suspect so, because Our Dumb Friends lobby is powerful the world over. Just you watch. When the boys from the London School of Economics eventually have Nelson off his plinth, I bet they won't dare lay hands on the Landseer lions. It was for this reason, I'm sure, that the Sudanese let Gordon on his camel come back intact from Khartoum, and who's to blame the children of Camberley for thinking that Gordon was the name of the camel? When I was a child I used to admire the two greyhounds that stood guard on either side of the gates outside the Beauchamp home near Norwich. They were, I now realise, the supporters from the family's coat of arms. Under them was the family motto, "Toujours fidèle" but I thought, in my innocence, that this was the name of the dogs, "Towzer and Fido". I hope these splendid animals have been well treated by the Regional Beetroot Board, or whoever it is now occupies the house.

On reflection I no longer want, nor, unless I am accompanied by some animal, deserve to have a statue erected to myself.

Winston's trousers will suffice.

When I left my home in Montagu Square I did go so far as to suggest to the LCC that they place on the house one of their round blue plaques saying "Lord Mancroft, Poet and Dreamer, born here". They replied by return of post explaining in some detail why this could not be. A previous letter from me complaining about the rates had on the other hand taken them nearly a month to answer. Next time I am worried about our dustbins I shall write, of course, to the Council, but I shall also propose by way of a postscript the erection of a statue to myself in Eaton Square. I bet the good fellows will reply to the whole letter within the day.

# 32

# Grand Hotels

ON THE top of the TV set in our hotel in Teheran stood a little notice. "In case of down break", it said, "please to send for Manager. Do not interfere with yourself."

I was happy to obey this instruction. Many hotels nowadays belong to some international conglomeration. They all look exactly alike, each one a more impersonal, albeit efficient, personal rest unit than the next. It was nice, therefore, to know that the Teheran hotel actually boasted anything so human as a Manager. I also remembered the occasion when I had asked to see the Manager of the Holiday Inn at Aruba off the coast of Venezuela. The little Dutch girl behind the counter obviously misunderstood me. "Sir," she said proudly, "We here are managed by a computer in Memphis, Tennessee."

Well, that's the way it is, and what with the growth of package holidays, and Conventions, not to mention the ordinary economic hazards of the hotel business, I'm afraid Mine Host with his smiling welcome may be on the way out.

Things were different when I was young. A few Grand Babylons were beginning to spring up, but by and large hotels in the 'twenties were still suited to their own particular purpose. Take, for instance, a commercial establishment like the delightful Station Hotel at Oswaldtwistle. While I yielded to none in my admiration for the art nouveau gas meters in the bedrooms, and its justly renowned Bovril en gelèe, it was frankly not the sort of place to which one would send the family for the whole of August.

People are now more exacting, and what with the tourist explosion, and the Jumbo jet, new hotels now have to be all things to all people for all seasons. The New Otani in Tokyo, for instance, is not just an hotel, it's an environment. It has a shopping precinct about the size of Croydon, and it has fourteen acres of garden. Our own Claridge's is proud of the fact that it has no bar. You simply ask someone for a drink just as you would ask the second footman in your own home. The New Otani, however, has thirteen bars, but asking for anything in that hotel can have surprising results. I phoned the hotel doctor and asked if I could have a cholera inoculation. We were bound next day for Hong Kong, where it is obligatory, and mine was out of date. I must have induced too urgent a note into my voice for within three minutes there was a pounding at our door, there stood the doctor in sinister gauze mask, accompanied by two orderlies with first-aid boxes, oxygen cylinders and stretchers, all demanding to know where the cholera victim was, and how long he had been infectious.

We flew with relief from the unpredictable efficiency of Tokyo to the kindlier expertise of The Mandarin Hotel in Hong Kong. The cherub who brought back my wife's dress from the valet showed no signs of withdrawing even after quite a comfortable tip. Was anything wrong? Indeed, no. The child then revealed why he was staying. "Zippy Missy up?" he inquired helpfully.

I think the Mandarin is one of the best hotels in the world, but here we are on contentious ground. The best hotel in the world is usually the one in which you are best known. That apart, I would before the War have voted for The Aviz in Lisbon. But now only its superb restaurant remains. Alberto Repetti, who owned and made it, died last year two days before I received his Christmas card. The Duke of Westminster once took a party there to lunch. "We must have something Portuguese," exclaimed Bend'or heartily. "In Aviz, your Grace," replied Repetti, "one doesn't must."

What others? Well, The Ritz, also in Lisbon, contends with The Ritz in Paris. The Ritz in London, despite its beautiful dining-room, alas, does not. The Gritti, in Venice; The Mount Nelson in Cape Town, where two little maids, in mob-caps still stand behind you at breakfast; The Plaza, in New York, or even our own dear Dorchester? All good pubs. I myself have a special regard for The Menzies, in Sydney, because it was there that I first encountered what was then a novel method of ordering your breakfast. You simply ticked off what you wanted on a card, and hung it on your door-handle over night. A former Bishop of Winchester, Dr. A. T. P. Williams, encountered it, too. His particular visit happened to coincide with a knitwear salesmen's Convention. The manager of the hotel realised what the brighter salesmen had been up to after hours when the night porter awoke him to say that he had an order from the Bishop to be called at 5 a.m. with 24 hard-boiled eggs and a bottle of rum—and was this right?

When I was with Cunard I used to resent the *QE2* being described as an hotel with a ship stuck on either end. On one occasion, however, we would have welcomed Repetti's advice. *QE2* went to the rescue of the French liner *Antilles* which had run aground and caught fire off the island of Mustique in the Caribbean. We took off 600 souls, including an elderly French lady who was understandably shaken by her experience. We wrapped her in blankets, trundled her along to the restaurant and gave her the best dinner we could muster. She appeared to enjoy it, sent for the headwaiter, and thanked him prettily. "But I hope you will not mind me mentioning", she said, "that the Sauce Béarnaise was just a little bit too thick."

A bit too thick indeed! You can say that again.

# 33

# Less grand hotels

THE CHAIRMAN, of course, will be staying at the Palace, the Savoia, the Grand, or the Kaiserhof. He's always stayed there, and his expense account is big enough.

A younger generation of chairmen stays at the Hilton, the Sheraton, the Intercontinental, or The Inn on the Park. The bill will be roughly the same, but the plumbing slightly quieter. It is, however, difficult to tell from the *décor*, when awakening in any of these caravanserai, whether you are in Tokyo, or Toronto, or Timbuktu. The bedrooms of most mass-produced hotels have roughly the same clinical anonymity. Downstairs we may find some distinctions. We can drink in The Pompadour Boudoir, The Crusaders' Mess, or The Barbarossa Bar, but upstairs the tooth-mugs have all been neatly sterilised for our especial protection.

Ah, but you aren't the chairman yet, are you? You've only just been appointed Assistant Overseas Marketing Manager of Better Mousetraps Ltd., and you're off to Ruritania (which recently joined the Common Market) to try and lift that contract from under the eyes of the wily foreigner. And where are you going to stay? Your position in the expense account pecking order doesn't yet rate a five-star hotel, and as this is your first visit to Ruritania you'd be wise to seek advice. Allow me to offer some.

To begin with you must, of course, stay in an hotel, and never in a private house. Yes, I know all about that charming Ruritanian couple you met at the company's last annual conference. They begged you to regard their home as yours when you were next in Ruritania, but this is a temptation to be resisted at all costs.

Towards the end of the war in Europe, Billy Butlin was instructed by H.M.G. to set up rest camps along the Belgian coast at Knokke and La Zoute for the recreation of the British soldiery on leave. Sir William applied himself to this task with his usual efficiency, but the scheme was a failure from the word go. No soldiers turned up. On their way along to Germany most of them had made friends with some kindly Dutch, Belgian or French family, and the moment their 48 hours leave came round, they turned straight back on their tracks, and had their feet under some table in next to no time. At least, I know I had mine.

Now, that's all very well in wartime, but it won't help you at all in your task of selling better mousetraps to the Ruritanians because your friends' house will lack two essentials. The first is a really efficient message desk, and the second is the ability to produce a hot bath at 4 o'clock in the morning, your plane having been delayed by threatened bombs, strikes, fog, and other acts of God. So we will now try to find you a small hotel where all essentials are readily at hand.

What's that you've got there? Oh, so you've been down to the Ruritanian National Travel office in Piccadilly, and picked up one of their hotel brochures, have you? Sensible chap, but you will remember, won't you, that it doesn't tell you where to stay: only offers subtle hints where not to stay. Take the Toisson d'Or, for instance. Reasonably priced, phone in every room, night porter, and all other mod. cons. But how could you guess that it is slap over the city's main railway station, and that you won't get a wink of sleep all night? You could, of course, have followed the example of the late A. E. Matthews who rang for the manager of his Birmingham hotel in the middle of the night and asked him what time the hotel reached Euston, but if you'd been a bit more experienced you'd have glanced at the map at the end of the brochure and seen that this situation was inevitable.

But who am I to preach? I was visiting Lisbon recently, and I chose a charming hotel from the map—reasonably priced, phone in every room, etc., and on the map, across the little street, a lovely blank space which I supposed was a cemetery, or an old people's rest home, the quiet sort of haunt where a mouse could have been heard sneezing. How was I to know that it was in fact the place where they printed Lisbon's leading newspaper? At 2 o'clock in the morning the noise sounded like a cross between the Battle of Alamein and the House of Commons at Question Time, neither of which is a suitable place for a mouse with a cold. You want to be careful about little streets, too. My favourite Paris hotel abuts on just such a one off the Bde des Italiens. It is ideal in every way unless you actually want to reach it, in which case stilts or roller-skates are required, so cluttered is it with the parked cars and juggernauts of the Common Market.

By now, of course, you have taken fright, and are thinking of applying for a transfer from Overseas Marketing to Home Admin. But have no fear—things are not as black as they seem. We have not yet really touched upon the best way of choosing an hotel, namely, that of personal recommendation. Before tackling the Ruritanian market for the first time your firm (if they know their business) will have sent you to discuss prospects with the Ruritanian desk at the Foreign and Commonwealth Office, the appropriate branch of the D.T.I., and, if they really want to make a meal of it, the Commercial Attaché at our Embassy in Ruritania, and our Consul-General in Zenda or Henzau. On quitting the presence you will inquire, with casual insouciance, "Oh, by the way, where ought I stay? The Eisener Hirsch, or the Colomba d'Oro perhaps, or even the Lion Bleu?" "What do you think I am?" asks old striped pants, a little petulantly, "a blooming travel agent?" But having appraised your problem correctly he will give you an equally correct solution.

You can confirm the wisdom of his choice by noting the speed with which the hotel confirms your booking and the standard of English in which it is couched. Very few good hotels, in any class, have a bad front office. The ultra-cautious will check again by phone the night before departure, since over-booking is an endemic disease in the travel world, and the Common Market with its outbreak of conferences will do nothing to relieve it. Tell MM. le Direction what time you plan to arrive so that they can get Herr Schmidt, or Senor Ruzziguzzi, out of your room before you yourself turn up, and ask them to reserve a corner for you in the bar where you can chat up your prospective customers in peace. If all goes well and you pull off the deal, your chairman will be delighted and you will be duly promoted. And next time you'll be allowed a suite at the Ritz.

One last piece of advice. Your Ruritanian opposite number may want to return your visit, and he may be as much in the dark about our hotels as you were about his. You mustn't lose face. You must be properly briefed. If you're a Londoner, like myself, you've probably never stayed in a London hotel—so you may want to play safe. Tell him, for instance, that by the end of 1974 there'll be fourteen hotels with over 8,000 bedrooms in the Heathrow area, which is more than they have in the whole of Wales, and all of which can provide for his every need. But don't let that stop him, of course, from visiting Wales when his business is over. Or, indeed, any other of the less familiar, less businesslike, and more beautiful parts of Britain.

Tell him in all truth that the standard of medium and small hotels in Britain has lately improved out of all recognition, and continues to do so.

But you'd better warn him that if he wakes up to the sound of pipes he's either in Scotland or something has gone wrong with the plumbing.

# 34

# The Officers' Mess

OUR COLONEL was addressing us in the reassuring tones of a man who knows that he has made a monumental boob.

"Chaps," he said, "there has been a misunderstanding. We have apparently marched five miles in the wrong direction and it will now be necessary for us to march ten miles back. If anyone feels unable to do this let him take three paces forward." The entire regiment took three paces forward with the exception of Bombardier Bean, who stood his ground. "I am proud," said the CO, "to find that one man at least in my regiment has the strength to undertake this arduous march. Well done, that man." "Sir," replied Bean sadly, "That isn't it. It's just that I haven't the strength to take three paces forward."

The tradition of the grand muddle is well established in the Army and will probably die hard. The good old Duke of York, for instance, not to mention his ten thousand men, experienced it at the top of the hill and also, of course, when HRH marched them down again.

Rupert of the Rhine, you will remember, thought Cromwell was a swine, and after Marston Moor he was quite sure. But Rupert was also a superb exponent of the art of military muddle, and it wasn't the fault of Old Noll that at Naseby Rupert issued orders which resulted in his two surviving squadrons charging each other full tilt during the climax of the battle. (Rupert himself was of course some miles away at the time.) And the Saxons had a general named, I think, Eggfilth, who misguidedly set up his GHQ in a quagmire outside Ipswich. As his troops passed by him in review he disappeared slowly and majestically from sight. This was muddle combined with panache. To an organisation as introspective as the Army, such things as the issue of 5,000 left boots to the 255 Battery RA must seem disconcerting to the layman, but it is something which any well brought up Quartermaster takes in his stride. There is, however, a logical reason for all this.

In days gone by we sent our bright boys into the law, into politics or diplomacy and we sent too many of our mutton-heads into the Army. Between major wars, we confined our defence policy to the ability to start a safe minor war if a suitable opportunity arose. The Army was not regarded as the profession for a serious man, and we all know what Wellington thought of "that article there". To me the surprise is that the article fought as well as he did. Siegfried Sassoon's General was a cheery old card, but he did for them all with his plan of attack. An additional target for criticism was the Staff, who were always at logger-heads with the troops at the front, and were alleged to have known nothing of the battlefields to which they were sending men to die. Hotspur said all there was to say about Staff Officers in Henry IV, Part 1, and as I went to the Staff College myself I've been re-reading Shakespeare to see in what way I too may have made confusion worse confounded.

Some while before going there, I had been sent to serve at Western Command HQ, and I had experienced there my first example of the Staff mind at its meticulous best. A document which I did not understand had passed one day through my In-tray. I duly initialled it and passed it on. It was returned to me later from the AQMG with a note saying I ought not to have seen it in the first place so would I please erase my initial and then initial the erasure.

What happens, I think, is this. Between wars we starve the

Army of men, money and material, and from bitter experience soldiers have learned to work on a shoe-string, and this leads to an over-meticulous ritual which can too easily tip over into absurdity. There is, however, a brighter side.

A little later in the recent conflict I was posted to the Military Operations Directorate of the War Office, and here a different situation prevailed.

I was immensely impressed by the skill and intellectual capacity of the Senior Officers under whom I had the honour to serve. The duds, of course, had been weeded out by then and the rest were picking up in the hard way the practical experience that cannot be gained in peace. Most of these officers had also been through the Staff College and in my opinion the Army has devised at Camberley a remarkably efficient system of instruction.

I myself, however, was there when improvisation and ad-hockery were still the order of the day. Liddell Hart points out in his History of the Second World War that though Monty was rightly renowned for the meticulous mounting of his set pieces, it is nevertheless in the art of improvisation that he especially excelled. I well remember the great man coming down to the Staff College and lecturing us on this particular aspect of his mystique. Courage was as essential in a soldier, he argued, as it was unnecessary in a man of business. In commerce, efficient planning should obviate the necessity of having to take any courageous decisions at all. Similarly, efficient administration ought to rule out the need for improvisation. For the soldier, however, who had to cope with the end product of political parsimony, improvisation was inevitable. I suspect that Monty had his tongue in his cheek when he expounded this doctrine, but he consoled us by concluding that we were bound in the end to win because God was on our side. I wanted to ask him whether he regarded the Almighty as being in support or under command, but I realised that such a question might be above my station.

Between lectures we students were sent out to umpire the

local Home Guard exercises. One such outing resulted in a shambles upon which neither Lord George-Brown, the Crazy Gang, nor the Marx Brothers could have improved. It fell to my lot to reprimand the platoon commander responsible. Just in time, I spotted a DSO and Bar half way down his second row of medals. I abated my flood of abuse. "Never mind, Sergeant," I said rather pompously, "better luck next time. I expect it's some while since you last commanded anything as humble as a platoon." "Sir," the old boy replied, "it's a long time since I last commanded anything." "Indeed, Sergeant," I asked, "and what was your last job in the Service?" He snapped to attention proudly, "Second Sea Lord, Sir."

Come to think of it the Senior Service can also make a pretty pudding of things, when they set their mind to it. Well, wouldn't you agree that it takes a fair amount of premeditation to run two battleships slap into each other in calm weather and in broad daylight as Admiral Tryon once managed to do with the *Victoria* and the *Camperdown*?

However, let us not pursue this line of thought too far because it only emphasises the national tendency to dwell on failures rather than on successes, and to pretend that defeats are really victories. Winston (with his own troubles at the Dardanelles in mind) gave voice to this danger at Dunkirk. And Field-Marshal Alexander echoed it as he prepared to leave the beaches. "Gentlemen," he observed, "I cannot bring myself to believe that this campaign is going in our favour."

This seems to me to strike the right balance between muddle and high courage. Lord Cardigan on the other hand went too far. He was of course a brave man though he brought a deeper and richer lustre to the meaning of the word cad. Who but he could have ridden back from leading the Charge of the Light Brigade to partake of champagne and a bath in his yacht in the harbour at Sevastopol?

That engagement must have been one of the most monumental muddles in the history of the British Army, but I'm afraid that Cecil Woodham-Smith dodges the issue when she called her superb description of it "The Reason Why". Not even she could explain convincingly why the muddle really occurred.

Perhaps we should spend less time worrying about the muddles that have inevitably occurred and a little more on congratulating ourselves upon the splendid way in which the British soldiery, considering how shabbily we, their employers, have treated them, have managed to overcome muddles, and do the country proud.

In all this I have an interest to declare because I have recently been appointed an Honorary Colonel Commandant in the Royal Artillery. This has occasioned me the greatest possible pride, especially when I recall that a CO once wrote in a report upon me that I was an officer whom the troops would follow anywhere, if only out of curiosity.

# 35

# Money out of leisure

HARKEN TO the words of Professor Folliot Scaramanga, Lecturer in Applied Sociology at the University of Pittsburg. (What *will* these Americans think of next, and what, incidentally, is *un*applied Sociology?)

The good Professor, like so many American savants, has been taking a long, hard look at the British economy. He has come to the conclusion that although most of us are now working a four-day week we still want five days in which to do it. If automation, and what the Prof. so neatly describes as the track-record rationalisation of endeavoural throughput, continue at its present pace we shall soon be working a three-day week, and eventually we shall have so much spare time on our hands that the only people who will be doing any work at all will be those whose job it is to provide for our leisure.

We shall, I suppose, still need a few essential non-leisure types like traffic wardens, undertakers, and the chaps who dig up main roads on bank holidays, but if we want our children to grow rich we should obviously be encouraging them to train for the leisure industry. They must become bunny girls, yacht hands and air-hostesses.

I'm afraid, however, there must be some flaw in this argument. How, otherwise, can you explain why our symphony orchestras are continually appealing for funds, why distinguished script-writers jostle each other round the doors of the Labour Exchanges, or why Carey Street is crowded with pop singers unready, willing, or able to pay their Income Tax?

Consider, also, the world of travel. There is no more obvious example of the growth of leisure than the current tourist explosion. Millions of people who have never ventured farther south than Bexhill are now winging their way to the Caribbean and the Costa Brava. The travel trade should therefore be in clover, but hardly any airline appears to be solvent, and many a package tour operator is selling matches in the Strand.

Next to travel there are few better ways of passing your leisure hours than in cultivating your garden. Some while ago, however, I was trapped by my head gardener into planting some onions, and the packet she gave me said Onions loudly and clearly. But, dammit, they have come up as petunias. Steak and onions; fine. But steak and petunias; h'm. I hope this isn't an occupational hazard in the seed merchants' world, because if it is, they may find it difficult to cash in to the full on this increasingly lucrative corner of the leisure market.

Come to think of it, I know very few rich actors, either. Miss Elizabeth Taylor (whom, unfortunately, I have never met) looks as smooth and as lush as the bijouterie which Mr. R. Burton sensibly plonked upon her, and she radiates a star quality which is nowadays all too rare. She is, however, hardly typical of the acting profession. The unemployment on the British stage and screen is deplorable, and this at a time when the standard of British acting is as high as it has ever been, and the demand for good theatre insatiable. A recent letter to the London Tourist Board gave Laurence Olivier's Shylock and breakfast at the Connaught Hotel as Britain's two finest cultural assets.

Consider next our pets. More leisure will enable us to spend more time with our little friends, and as we all know to our cost the doggy/pussy business is big. I've just learned, however, that a lot of what Fido eats seems to be whale-meat, and the

Whale Protection Society doesn't much care for this because the world is apparently running out of whales. I don't know what they'll put into the tins if the poor whales do eventually pack up altogether.

Keen market men will obviously think up something new, but they mustn't upset the balance of nature. You know how it is. You have a plague of locusts in L'bomboland. Then some boffin comes along with a new and wonderful drug, which puts paid to the locusts. But it upsets the balance of nature, and before you know where you are you're landed with a surfeit of wart-hogs in Wolverhampton. So the man who can find a suitable stand-in for whales has got a fortune on his hands if he's careful.

I also suspect that there's a risk of us upsetting the balance between leisure and work. Pretty soon leisure's going to become work, and the people who will make money out of our increased leisure won't be the actors, violinists, jockeys, ghillies, croupiers, strip-tease artistes, and repairers of smashed windows on football excursion trains, but the middlemen who can make money out of them.

Take betting for instance. Here I must declare an interest because I happen to be chairman of the Tote Board, and, along with the bookies, I naturally hope that more leisure will bring more punters onto the race-courses. But successful gambling, if you want to make money out of jackpots, Yankees, trebles, and similar sophistications, is beginning to look less like leisure and more like work for a senior wrangler. The successful punter is a very hard-working man.

In fact I don't think you and I are going to make much money out of any of the old-fashioned leisure markets. I realise that Mr. Henry Cooper has become a name at Lloyds (and quite right, too) but by and large it's the promoters and not the boxers who will make such money as is still to be made out of a dying sport. All-in wrestlers will not get rich as quickly as the managers who rehearse them. Steer clear also of cricket—a game which the English, not being a spiritual people, have invented in order to give themselves some conception of Eternity. And cricket, because of the dearth of star players, is also a dying sport, and unsuitable for the up and coming entrepreneur.

What in fact we've got to do if we really want to make money out of leisure is to find something completely new with which to unjade the public palate. There will obviously be difficulties about reintroducing public executions, and the same applies to the stocks and the pillory. The announcement of a bull-fight at Wembley would probably produce a queue which would stretch from the box-office to the moon, but there might be Questions in Parliament. We must therefore stay within the Law.

As the computer takes over our daily lives, so a good pair of hands will become rarer and rarer. Self-service and do-it-yourself are the order of the day. Service then is something of which the British seem to have become a little suspicious. When and where did you last have your car properly serviced? Have you ever tried to find a plumber, or a dentist, on a Sunday? Many women regard shopping as a hobby, like bingo or bridge, and it worries them that so many shop assistants are frankly upset if you ask them to sell you anything. We have, alas, nearly a million unemployed, but in most good restaurants the waiters no speaka da English. They are eager, however, to give a service in which the British are largely uninterested, and then, having learned the trade and the tricks thereof, they and their family set up on their own in the Ristoranti Ptomaino in some remote territory like Barons Court.

It seems, therefore, that it will be out of servicing other people's leisure that the real money is going to be made. I ran into an old Gunner friend of mine the other day in New York. He had commanded a battery in my regiment, and had done it very well, too. He's now working as butler/handyman to some tycoon on Long Island, and his wife backs him up as cook/housekeeper. They have a flat, a car, coloured TV, their own scrubbing lady, and six weeks' holiday a year. And they earn about the same as the Lord Chancellor, and everybody just adores their English accent.

I saw recently an advertisement in the *New York Times* for just such a couple. They were required to look after a retired beef baron in San Antonio, Texas. Well, admittedly, I'm not all that good at folding jackets, but I'm quite clever at polishing shoes and cleaning silver; I can regulate clocks, mend fuses, and I can hand round the soup without sloshing it unduly. My wife, though I have not yet seen fit to show her the advertisement, is a good cook if nobody watches, a superb gardener, and a dab hand on the typewriter as long as we give her a machine that can spell.

And we both have *adorable* English accents.

# 36

# Unearned money

"YOU'LL LIKE Palm Beach," they said. "If God had only had money He'd have made Palm Beach Himself."

They were right, too. It's a wonderful place, and over the whole neighbourhood there wafts a delicious smell—the smell of unearned income. We sat sniffing it outside the Country Club, that outward and visible sign of American social success, Mrs. Rosenkranz bore down upon us. She, too, was visibly significant with her blue-rinse, her rimless glasses, and her mottled claws clanking with gold. Behind her came Mr. Rosenkranz, skinny legs protruding from Bermuda shorts, white cap over his eyes, and a cigar clamped firmly between his jaws. He was clutching a basket from which protruded the *US News & World Report*, the *Wall Street Journal*, and momma's suntan lotion. From time to time Mrs. Rosenkranz looked back and issued that call of the All-American matriarch, "Come, Elmer." Elmer naturally came.

From the other side of the patio Mrs. Guildenstern emerged. She was alone, being at the moment between husbands. I was told that she already supported three exes, not to mention four homes, and five charities, the officials of which would have been in serious personal trouble if it had not been for her interest in their respective causes. Her father had made his money out of bubble-gum, which one was not allowed to mention in her presence. (Balzac says that behind every great fortune is a great crime; but I'm sure he can't have been thinking of bubble-gum.)

Both ladies had one thing obviously in common. Neither of them appeared to be enjoying herself. The face of each displayed all the softness and expressive mobility of an empty cigar box. Rich people the world over tend to look unhappy, and if the two ladies ever come over to Britain and start living it up in Torquay or Gleneagles they will probably look unhappier still.

In America they realise, as we do, that great inequalities of wealth breed great injustice. They are not particularly proud of the way some of their oil-men and movie magnates made their money between the wars and as their reaction to the tragedy at Chappaquiddick indicated, they no longer think that there should be one law for the rich and another for the very rich. Nevertheless, Americans are still more interested in creating wealth than they are in soaking the rich. They do not regard profit or inheritance as dirty words, and they do not understand the Socialist policy of getting up in the middle of the night and stealing the money out of your own trouser pockets. They may therefore be puzzled by the pamphlet, *Labour's Economic Strategy* (price 15p post free from Transport House). So, frankly, am I.

This work concentrates on the current theory that fiscal policy should be less concerned with the raising of revenue than with the settling of old political scores. Envy, hatred and malice are, of course, wonderful vote-catchers. Not content, therefore, with higher surtax, a dividend freeze, an extension of the capital gains tax, recurring once-for-all capital levies, and further measures against the mitigation of death duties, the authors of this pamphlet now promise us not only a gift tax but a wealth tax, too. Let us soak the rich with a vengeance, and if possible soak their sons as well. Any new ideas for actually creating wealth seem to have been submerged in a mulish disapproval of the hereditary principle. What also seems to have been overlooked is the fact that the creation of wealth must of necessity concentrate assets in the hands of a minority. Suppose no wealth of any sort could be inherited. Wealth would then be concentrated in the hands of people at the point of retirement who had accumulated savings out of their income during their working lives. And a fat lot of good that would do anyone.

I can understand the Leftist dislike of the hereditary principle, though for my part I believe there's more to be said for it than is now fashionable to admit. Herbert Morrison once remarked ruefully, after a tactical defeat at the hands of Lord Salisbury, that he must in future remember that the Noble Marquis had been at the game four hundred years longer than he had.

I also realise that some people do genuinely regard money as the root of all evil. But once you've overcome this basic objection, where precisely lies the distinction between earned and unearned income. Is it really an immoral thing that a man should want his son to have a better start in life than he did? Oughtn't it to make him work harder, seek promotion, and keep away from bookies and blondes? And, surely, to tax pensions and savings as if they were unearned income is not only silly but unjust.

During the war there was a tiresome policy of denying leave to the boys in Theatre A because it wasn't possible to give it to the boys in Theatre B. This was regarded by the War Office as a fine example of official fair play, and by the boys in both Theatres as plain daft. The same logic now inspires the Chancellor. If Tom's and Dick's dads can't leave them any money, then Harry's, who can, isn't going to be allowed to do so either. A complicated and inequitable system of taxation has been created to see that he doesn't. Family arrangements that have been legal for years are declared illegal over night. A multitude of lawyers and accountants, who could be better employed in something a little more constructive, spend their time in devising schemes to diddle the Treasury. And thousands of civil servants have to spend their time, and our money, in devising schemes to diddle the diddlers, who, because they regard the law as basically unfair, do not think there is anything improper in what they are doing.

All men are born equal, but fortunately quite a few of them soon get over it. If those few were allowed to inherit a little of father's money they might possibly put it to good use, and make it create more wealth. But what about those who have stayed equal, who were not actually failures but merely started at the bottom and liked it there? Well, a fool and his money are soon parted, and if it's caused by drinking and gambling, then most of the money will eventually come back to the state in taxes. That ought to satisfy those who don't think a fool and his money should ever be allowed to come together in the first place.

Those who regard this pamphlet as no more than preliminary electioneering should consider the doctrine of the Unbalanced Pendulum. The old theory of alternative government (the swing, that is, of the political pendulum) only works when neither party threatens the fundamental interests of its political opponents. In all its years of government the Conservative party destroyed nothing which Socialists care about. State schools, the welfare state, trade unions, workingmen's clubs, even the nationalised industries themselves were all left untouched. And I'm willing to bet that most Socialists actually become richer under the Tories.

The Labour party on the other hand is not only dedicated to the irrevocable destruction of Tory institutions and ideas, but, as we can clearly see, to the impoverishment of individual Tories as well. The whole idea of a wealth tax, with its implied attack on inheritance, is yet another contribution to the politics of envy, and if, thanks to their dislike of unearned income, the Socialists do manage to ruin a successful private business, or send the family pictures into Sotheby's, the return of a Tory government won't put matters to rights. Unfortunately the pendulum is not balanced that way. Even if the Socialists lose the next election we can't just sit back and hope that no harm has been done. The Left doesn't have to win elections to do damage. Some of the harm that a wealth tax does can be caused by the mere threat of its arrival. The brain drain may soon become a flood. The flight of capital could accelerate, and in an attempt to check it the currency regulations may get stiffer and sillier. What encouragement is there for new investment, or for the building up of new enterprises? And think of the hardship that may fall upon those whose "wealth" is in a form which generates no income to pay the tax.

Although the pamphlet may boost the sale of Premium Bonds, which can incidentally, generate a deal of unearned income, it is also an attack on the whole concept of savings. It is even an attack on the whole concept of thrift, and, like Mesdames Rosenkranz and Guildenstern, I revere thrift—particularly in an ancestor.

# 37

# Spending money in style

THE WIDOW, when she spent her mite, at least spent it in style.

The Prodigal Son, on the other hand, wasted his substance with riotous living, but whether or not he did this in style is uncertain. No tales have come down to us of rejoicing with the daughters of the Philistines in Gath, nor (perish the thought) has anything been published about triumphing with the daughters of the uncircumcised in the streets of Askelon. Nevertheless, the Prodigal Son had to fall back on pig swill for luncheon, which must have been very embarrassing for a nice Jewish boy like him.

I myself have mixed feelings about money. It doesn't, of course, buy friends, though it does allow you a better class of enemy, and there are few sorrows, however poignant, in which a good income can be of no avail. Money is the sixth sense that helps you to enjoy the other five. It would therefore be nice if Providence could think less about money itself, and more about the sort of people to whom it is given. Any fool can make money, but spending it in style is more difficult. In the cash box the dividing line between style and banality is finely drawn.

Diamond Jim Brady used to light his cigar with a dollar bill, and that was very bad style indeed. It's vulgar and pointless, and the smell of burning dollar bills would probably ruin even an American cigar. But Diamond Jim redressed the balance when he sent Lilian Russell three dozen roses each containing a diamond in place of the customary dew-drop. That, I think, was charming, and it stops just short of ostentation. Four dozen would have spoilt the whole thing, as sheer size so often does.

For instance, you've really got to have the taste of a Sun King to inject style into anything like as grandiose as Versailles. And for this reason I'm reserving judgement on the Cheops boys and their pyramids, and on Solomon in all his rather brazen glory. I am, however, glad that Solomon had the wisdom not to marry that flashy Queen of Sheba. Nobody has to work so hard for his money as the man who's married it.

Pugnacious spending can be bad for style. You mustn't buy Renoirs just to trump your neighbour's Cezannes. And don't let your wife go alone to Yves St. Laurent's place in Paris. Women can seldom buy clothes in style when they are alone, because they seldom dress to please either men or themselves. They dress to annoy other women.

Revengeful spending, however, can have style. Lord Nuffield once wanted to join a certain golf club, but some of the members objected. So he bought the whole club, and only elected the members who had smiled upon him. I think that's nice.

There can, of course, be as much style in the reasons for spending money as there is in the spending itself. I remember once sitting next to Bud Flanagan at a charity auction, and I praised the generosity of those who were pushing up the bids. "Nonsense," Bud snorted. "Conscience Money. None of them has put in a proper tax return for years."

I hope the same principle doesn't apply to those who spend money on building new libraries, or endowing Chairs of Chiropody. Unkind people suggest that this may also be done to ensure that the Princess will actually come to their daughter's dance, or that they may eventually trump their neighbour's Knighthood with a Peerage. I'm sure this can't be so! That's no better than giving the headwaiter a fat tip as you come into the restaurant in order to guarantee service to come. That's a bribe rather than a tip, and it's the negation of spending in style.

Mark you, tipping can be a test for any stylist. You needn't be a millionaire to do it well, but you've got to have panache. I recall with affection the standards set by my friend, Charlie Cringleford, who was up at The House with me in the thirties. He was by no account a rich man, but he was a very pretty spender all the same. When he was in the Army he used to send his shirts home every week from India to be washed. And his soldier servant once found a note on the dresser saying, "Please put two bottles of the Cockburn '12 by my bedside, and call me the day after tomorrow."

When he was at Oxford Charlie had been the proud owner of a Morgan run-about. It was, despite the Dean's disapproval, called God, because it moved in a mysterious way. Everything about the car made a noise except the horn, and it did about two telegraph poles to the gallon with the wind behind it.

Well, one evening Charlie was bidden to a smart rout at Londonderry House. He drove up to the front door in this bizarre vehicle, resplendent in top hat, white tie and tails. "Shall I park it for you, M'lord?" asked the linkman. "No, no," said Charlie loftily, "keep it for yourself, my good man. By all means, keep it," and he strolled through the front door peeling off his white kid gloves.

At this point I should declare my own preference. I am not interested in cars, or chiropody, and, although I shall have my ears boxed for saying so, I think Renoir is an over-rated artist.

On the other hand I greatly admire Sir Joseph Camps, who may possibly not be known to you. He it was who refused to accompany Captain Cook on his trip to Australia unless he was allowed to take with him not one but two horn players to entertain him during dinner. There's richness for you! But when my football pools come home I shall blue the proceeds not just on two horns but on a whole private orchestra.

Of course I realise there's nothing very original about this. Nebuchadnezzar did it with his cornet, flute, harp, sackbut, psaltery, dulcimer, and all the other kinds of music to be found in Daniel 3. v.5, and a pretty cacophonous combo that must have been. I have mixed feelings, too, about the Emperor Meiji whose Court musician once composed a Concerto for 24 Japanese singing-mice and a bass trombone. Unfortunately, at the first run through the trombone inhaled an alto singing-mouse, and the whole project had to be abandoned. Nevertheless, the basic idea was sound.

The German princelings of the eighteenth century were no great shakes as rulers, but Bach, Handel and Haydn started on their way to fame and Paradise with the Grand Duke's little drawing-room band. My band will be private, but far from little, and whether the players like it or not I shall conduct it myself. I was once allowed to conduct the Bonn University Student orchestra, and a maggotty-headed lot of layabouts I thought they were. Would you believe it, by the time I'd got as far as bar 200 in the last movement of Beethoven's 7th they'd got no further than bar 182? I had to bring them up pretty sharply on no less than three occasions, but on the third the leader said that if I did it again they'd play exactly as I was conducting.

I realise, of course, that a private orchestra costs the earth. Indeed, if you have to ask how much, you obviously can't afford one. Like a yacht. And, talking of yachts, did any prime minister ever disport himself in greater style than Mr. Heath in *Morning Cloud II*? It's all very well for Mr. H. Wilson to grumble, but let's wait and see how he spends the proceeds of his Memoirs. Dr. Johnson spent the money he earned from the first number of *The Rambler* on oysters for Hodge his cat. If Mr. Wilson can show greater style than that I'll eat my hat. Even if I have to buy one specially for the job, I'll eat it—and in style.

# 38

# Collector's pieces

WE, (that is, the Assistant Secretary of the Winchester College Archaeological Society, together with a certain Mlle. Fifi de la Bon-Bon and I) were all sitting in the lounge bar of the South Western Hotel at Southampton drinking port and lemon. The occasion was a routine half-holiday visit by the Assistant Secretary and myself to the ships then lying in Southampton Docks. A benevolent Housemaster, approving our interest in the Merchant Marine, always encouraged such expeditions. As evidence, however, that our interest had been properly exercised we were required to bring back with us a picture postcard of every ship that we had visited, duly signed by the officer of the Watch.

Mlle. Fifi (née Sally Scroggs) was at the time appearing at the Southampton Hippodrome where, twice nightly, she took off her clothes slowly and courteously to music. As experienced ship-visitors we had provided for a little time in hand and were thus able to demonstrate our preference for her company over that of the second officer of the S.S. *Ascania*. Unfortunately, on presenting our postcards for the Housemaster's perusal that evening, we carelessly omitted to remove from the collection a signed photo of Fifi wearing only three small bits of elastoplast and a dignified smile. That was the end of our visits to the docks and of my own excellent collection of ship postcards.

I was reminded of all this when I was invited by the Postcard Association of Great Britain to open an exhibition in celebration of their Centenary. I had no idea what an enormous range and variety has been produced over the years and I was delighted to renew acquaintance with old favourites such as Donald McGill's bright pink sea-side ruderies. How simple they seem in comparison with the pictures of John Lennon and Yoko Ono in the nude which you can now buy in Piccadilly Circus if you are so minded.

There were also of course the inevitable views of the Tower and the Abbey to send back to Cousin Flo whom you haven't bothered to see for years, and duly inscribed "Wish you were here"; but a right nasty shock you'd get if the old bird took you at your word and suddenly turned up. And would you believe it, they now even make narrow scenic picture postcards to fit inside goldfish bowls so that the fish think they're going places.

One member of the Postcard Collectors Club told me that he had no less than 40,000 cards in his collection and all in albums too. This astonished me because whilst I, being interested in ships, collected ship postcards, he just collected postcards. This seems to me to be a collection complex run riot and I find it difficult to analyse. Perhaps his mother had been frightened by a magpie or a squirrel just before he was born.

Stamps and coins I can understand because they have both historical interest and financial value. Cigarette cards and matchbox covers also have their admirers. Miniature bottles of rare and dangerous aperitifs look pretty but they collect the dust and make an atrocious mess if you accidentally overdust them. I greatly envy a Mr. Comus Elliott of Braintree who collects pubs. He claims to have drunk a pint of beer in over 5,000 different houses. Lovely! And of course this collection doesn't take up any room which is one of the great snags with collecting in the grand manner. You'd need a house about the size of Blenheim to store 40,000 albumed postcards in proper style.

The late Genghis Khan used to collect the left ears of gentlemen whom he had defeated in battle or who had otherwise put him out. How on earth did he store them? I mean, you can't just walk into Boots and ask for a nice left ear album, please.

My own collecting habits are more modest and are confined to swizzle sticks, book-matches and hotel bedroom notices saying "Do not disturb" in a wide variety of languages. I insist for my own self-discipline that they must have been obtained by me first hand in the normal course of business and no presentations, however lush and tempting, are acceptable. It is now a pretty classy collection, and it is pleasant on a wet and windy night in Wiltshire to ruffle through the pack and recollect a muscular Rum Punch drunk in the sea off Negril in Jamaica, or to remind oneself how impossible it is to be left undisturbed in any hotel in Florida. This is because the maid automatically opens your bedroom door at 8 a.m. muttering "Room Check". (Actually it's not a room check at all; it's a you check.)

The most talented collector in our family was my Uncle Bertie. He specialised in water-colours, vintage port and blondes. Aunt Maud admired John Sell Cotman and on a cold day liked a drop of the Cockburn '04. But she didn't know about the blondes until she accidentally came across Uncle Bertie collecting a well-packaged specimen behind the conservatory at our local Church fête. Aunt Maud was neither blonde nor well-packaged. She was a bluntly built woman with an outlook to match, and poor Uncle Bertie was told to eject this particular item from his collection at once, or else.

He then took to collecting corkscrews and had acquired a fine range by the time my children misguidedly gave him for Christmas a corkscrew which was driven by compressed air. Uncle Bertie was not mechanically minded and must presumably have failed to note that the ratchet marked A was not firmly inserted behind the toggle bars marked B & C. Anyhow, there was a fearful explosion and we all rushed into the library to find Uncle lying on his back under the piano, plucking plastic tubing out of his moustache and making ungrateful remarks about my children.

I suppose that at the bottom of all collecting there is an element of snobbishness, a sense of one-upmanship. The collector of swizzle sticks and book-matches has been to more exotic places than you have. The same underlying principle applied to the Edwardian ladies who collected scalps and hunted lions. It applies also to those who collect foreign decorations—the Grand Cross of Gingivitis perhaps, or even the Ruritanian Order of Chastity (fourth class).

We had a French Liaison Officer in Normandy who sported about nine rows of ribbons. Our padre fancied himself an expert on the subject but even he had to confess that two of Marcel's gongs defeated him. "Well, Padre," Marcel explained helpfully. "As you know, I served for some time between the wars in the Protectorate of Gombolie. This medal here was for putting it across the Sultan's wife and this, next to it, was for putting it across the Sultan. Very rare."

For me and my ship postcards the wheel has now come full circle. Just after the war when Cunard had twelve passenger ships in the fleet we used to get through nearly half a million postcards in a year. Passengers, people coming aboard at ports, and other assorted magpies and squirrels, used to stuff their pockets full of them. Where collecting ends and acquiring begins is not always easy to define. So now Cunard make people ask for postcards if they want them. This was unpopular at first, but not so unpopular as designing the *QE2* coathangers with a ball and fixed socket at the top which, of course, is of no use in the home. Before we did this we used to have about 25,000 coathangers collected off us every year. Fortunately I collected my coathangers off Cunard before I joined the firm.

# 39

# Boating about in messes

AT THE week-ends I go down to the country to an old Cotswold malt-house a few miles from where the Thames rises. And a very pretty sight that is, too. You can sit on a bank whereon the wild thyme really does grow, and you can watch the twenty yard old Thames gurgling and sploshing away in preparation for its 210 mile journey down to The Nore. Unfortunately, the journey doesn't always bring us much credit.

Things don't begin too badly. Past Lechlade, only a few miles from its source, the river has already grown surprisingly big; big enough, in fact, to harbour one or two of the few remaining Thames barges. Less surprisingly there is also a goodly company of canoes, skiffs, dinghies, cabin-cruisers, fireflies, and boats of all sorts, the messing about in which, as Ratty informed his old friend Mole in "The Wind in the Willows", there was nothing, absolutely nothing, half so much worth doing as.

I'm glad, however, that Ratty and Mole aren't with us on some week-days when, weather permitting, members of the House of Lords step out from the Lords' Chamber onto the Terrace at Westminster. Sweet Thames, alas, is no longer running as softly as the poet Spenser wished. It has now become a turgid, smelly old sewer, and Ratty and Mole, instead of messing about in boats, would find themselves boating about in messes of which we and they ought to be thoroughly ashamed.

A dirty old board was once drifting under Westminster Bridge, and one Civil Servant asked another what it could be. His friend admitted ignorance of the matter, but suggested unkindly that it plainly couldn't be the Board of Inland Revenue because it was actually moving.

Amongst its many achievements the London Tourist Board has at last made people realise that the Thames is a beautiful and historic thoroughfare, and not just a useful drain. We are, in fact, all now becoming river minded. And about time, too.

The G.L.C. has produced an 85-page booklet setting out its views. Lady Dartmouth has said her piece. A barrage is to be built at Woolwich which will make it safe for Ratty and Mole to mess about from Coln St. Aldwyns to Canvey Island. Sir A. P. Herbert, who first campaigned for the barrage, will cheer his head off in the watery Paradise to which the Walkyrie of Hammersmith have rightly carried him. A former Lord Mayor of London, Sir Peter Studd, has plans to brighten up the riverside, and the 1975 Outdoor Lighting Awards Committee are organising competitions. Upstream the local authorities are telling their coke-lighters that they must look to their manners, and downstream the planners at Maplin are even starting to worry about the comfort of the geese who have hitherto honked there unmolested.

All the same, I still can't help wondering who actually dumps all that rubbish in the Thames—the flotsam (which, as you know, floats) and the jetsam (which, of course, sinks). Who else messes about in boats on the river, and might possibly have a guilty conscience?

It can't be Oxford and Cambridge because their eights have no room for rubbish, and in any case we needn't worry about them because their annual race will soon disappear for lack of public support. It can't be the excursion launches run by Mr. Walter Caisley and his friends during the few months in the year that weather permits because they are always maintained in a way that would make the *QE2* look to her laurels. I hope, too, we can excuse the fire-boats, the police boats, the *Cutty Sark*, and H.M.S. *President*. The big liners have stopped messing about at Tilbury, and have nearly all moved to Southampton. St. Katherine's Dock is closing down, and they're replacing it with hotels, conference halls, and (wake up Ratty and Mole) a yachting marina. The Surrey Docks will soon be closing down as well, for want of business. So that'll be another potential rubbish-dump out of the way.

The water-taxis which could do so much to ease London's traffic problems have, for some odd reason, never yet got going. So they can't be the culprits. A few genuine canal barges still ply their trade where the river links with the Grand Union Canal. But they are as meticulously clean and tidy as are the myriads of children who live aboard them. Incidentally, have you ever wondered why bargees have such big families? I have, but it's just been explained to me that it's difficult to dodge in a barge.

It looks, then, as if there's a possibility that from lack of trade as much as from growing conscience the river may soon be a little cleaner—fit even for salmon and trout, who are fussier than us humans. But will it be any safer? Many famous artists have been attracted to the Thames and rightly so, but if you study the works of Canaletto, Monet, Derain and Whistler, to name only a few, you will find their pictures all have one thing in common—they are full of little boats whizzing all over the place without any regard for the rules of the river. This may just be artistic licence, but if not, and if our boating population is going to increase in the way the planners hope, riparian life may soon become very haphazardous.

In August 1924 Maj. the Hon. E. E. Cringleford was hauled up before the Beaks for flying his aeroplane under Tower Bridge. In his defence he stated that he made a habit of flying under bridges because you met a better class of people there—the yachting crowd, and so on.

If we're going to tidy up the river, and build more yacht harbours and marinas, well and good. But we'd better also tidy up our knowledge of elementary navigation, or the Thames will become as dangerous in the future as it was dirty in the past.

Ratty and Mole please note. We have our eye on you.

# 40

# Revenge

ONE AFTERNOON, shortly before the war, I was strolling up St. James's Street with my father who had an embarrassing sense of humour. We had got as far as Pope, Roach, the chemists, when he seized me by the arm and marched me into the shop, which happened to be pretty full. "Excuse me," he said, pitching his voice on a note of paternal alarm, "my little boy here has ringworm. Would you advise me to put brimstone in his cocoa?"

Even now, I blush to recall the resulting uproar. To a young man of twenty-two who was beginning to fancy himself as a bit of a blade, the situation was, to say the least of it, unwelcome. This, however, was not the first occasion upon which I had fallen victim to this particular trick and I thought therefore, it was time I taught my father a lesson.

Revenge came my way more swiftly than I had hoped, or my father had probably expected. Next day, pausing in front of the window of Partridges, I suddenly feigned interest in a fine Sheraton escritoire, and lured my father inside. An exquisite person approached us, holding his hands as if in prayer. "My uncle, up from the country," I said, "is looking for a good secondhand bird's-eye maple commode. Do you think you could possibly oblige the old fellow?"

Skimming later through the twelfth chapter of St. Paul's Epistle to the Romans, it dawned upon me that I ought not to have taken this sort of revenge on my poor old father because "vengeance is mine", saith the Lord, and (He addeth) "I will repay". I realise of course that things must have been pretty tough for the early Christians in Rome at the time of writing, what with lions, boiling oil, gridirons, and so on. A firm direction by St. Paul was therefore obviously in order, particularly since the Bible's guidance is confusing. What, for instance, about an eye for an eye and a tooth for a tooth? What about Naboth's vineyard? And weren't the Prophets of Baal handed out a very well deserved comeuppance by Elijah? Frankly, then, I feel that St. Paul was justified with his recap of Deuteronomy XXVII, v. 35, because the lesson had obviously not been well observed in days gone by.

One can also see why Juvenal remarked that revenge was sweet, just as one can also see that it's not always very attractive. One of the nastiest photographs taken during the war showed Hitler dancing an obscene little jig when he was told that Paris had fallen. A few days later Keitel and Jodl ushered the vanquished French into a *wagon-lit* in the forest of Compiègne and there submitted them to the same humiliation that their own forebears had undergone at the hands of the French in 1918. Such a thing was bound to happen—you could see retribution like that sticking out a mile.

This is one of the awkward things about revenge: it must breed counter-revenge, particularly, of course, in war. I don't know what's happened to that ill-omened *wagon-lit*, but I secretly hope it's been moved to another part of the forest, or lost, or burnt, or accidentally shunted down to Clermont-Ferrand, or somehow moved out of temptation's way before it starts putting ideas into another generation's head. (If all this fails, it could possibly be brought over to England and used as a football special between Leeds and Manchester—that would wreck it completely.)

Revenge, must also contain some element of poetic justice.

Merely getting your own back is not good enough. We're on safe ground, for instance, with Baron Humphrey de Bohun who, discovering that his vintner was supplying him with adulterated plonk, had the wretched man boiled alive in a vat of his own medicine. That, I think, is neat.

The Borgias, of course, are in a class by themselves when it comes to getting one's own back. Roderigo Borgia, after he became Pope Alexander VI and had presumably found time to have a look at Romans XII v. 19, remarked that the Almighty must have realised that vengeance was a bit too sweet for man, and had therefore kept it for His own tooth. When he was only a cardinal, Roderigo had a less resigned approach. Finding, once, that his current mistress had become over-confidential with her confessor, he had them both nailed up in their confessional box in the cathedral at Segovia and this must have given the rest of the congregation quite a bit to chat about during the duller parts of the sermons.

I am sure the Borgias would have approved of a device thought up by the Australians at Gallipoli. Taking exception to some particularly devious Turkish ploy, the Aussies began lobbing over their Mills grenades with the fuses reversed and the pins undrawn. The Turks, thinking the simple Australians had forgotten to draw the pins, did so themselves before preparing to lob the grenades back and were blown to smithereens for their pains. That one was both neat and gaudy. So too was the action of some American soldiers at Sackett's Harbour in the war of 1812. They were fired upon by a British ship and our cannon balls unfortunately fell short. The Americans picked them up, loaded them into their own guns, fired back, scored a direct hit and sank our ship. This was as near to being hoist with your own petard as doesn't matter.

Similar feelings were displayed in the recent contest. Even the biblical-minded Monty must have overlooked Romans XII, v. 19 when he sent London troops up into the Pas de Calais to capture the German flying-bomb sites. Those infernal machines were still landing on London homes with a weight and regularity that was nearly bringing London to its knees. Many of the British 2nd Army troops had already lost their families in flying-bomb raids, and they set about their task of demolishing the rocket sites from which the bombs were launched with (literally) a vengeance.

Leaving aside my father and the bird's-eye maple commode, I think I have only one matter still on my own conscience, and that was not for any revenge I took, but for one I deliberately did not.

After the war, and before my demob, I found myself behind a desk in Belgium, thinly disguised as a GSO 1. Among my many and onerous duties was the granting of priority air passages to those officers and men who wanted to go home to get their businesses reorganised before their rivals could beat them to it. Into my office there walked one day a skinny and unprepossessing subaltern with a beaky nose, in search of just such a permit. He asked if by chance I remembered him. I did, by golly, though obviously he had forgotten why. He had been at Winchester with me and a horrible bully he was too. This was at a time when, as readers of Nicholas Montserrat's autobiography will recall, Winchester had a perfectly dreadful reputation for cruelty. I reminded Beaky Nose of this, and of the contribution he himself had made towards that reputation. I reminded him in some detail, in unrefined language, and in front of the other ranks, which is, of course, unpardonable. I commented also upon the modest rank he had himself attained and in a very mediocre unit at that. I touched lightly upon the understandable failure of his marriage and the probable failure of his business. I went over this ground several times and with embellishments. In short, I behaved abominably.

I think that Beaky Nose was genuinely upset. He clearly did not remember how badly he had behaved twenty years back and this, I told him, only made matters worse. He must, by then, have obviously come to the conclusion that he was getting no priority air-ticket out of me.

For my own part, however, I decided to forego revenge. In

taking revenge, says Bacon, a man is but even with his enemy, but in passing it over, he is his superior. I determined, therefore, to heap coals of fire on my beaky-nosed enemy. I signed his permit with a flourish and I flicked it contemptuously across the table.

That evening in the Mess, I learned to my horror that his plane had crashed on take-off and that there had been no survivors.